Foreword

UPTOWN DOWN SOUTH is a collection of menus that is the culmination of a five-year project of the Junior League of Greenville, Inc. The more than 400 triple-tested recipes are arranged in menus that take you from morning to midday and into the evening. Ranging from the uptown elegance of gourmet dinners and cocktail parties to down south casual dining on the patio or tailgating before the game, each menu has been planned with special attention to taste, appearance and recipe compatibility.

The rationale behind the menu format of UPTOWN DOWN SOUTH was to develop a book to help today's hostess and family chef streamline entertainment and meal preparation. Many of our menus highlight traditional holidays, family gatherings and social occasions enjoyed everywhere, with serving suggestions or decorating ideas. UPTOWN DOWN SOUTH goes a step beyond the standard by offering glimpses of our lifestyle in Greenville, South Carolina. By featuring historical aspects of Greenville, along with cultural, social and community events, we have tried to share some of the uptown advantages and down South amenities Greenville offers.

Just as the recipes and menus here are a collection of old and new, traditional and contemporary, so is life in Greenville. The heritage and opportunities that keep many native sons and daughters here, also serves to continually bring new families to our community. The result is a progressive community that still maintains the best of its relaxed friendly southern atmosphere.

We hope that you will find UPTOWN DOWN SOUTH an indispensable cookbook in your collection and that through these pages you will savor not only the flavor of our menu ideas but also what they reflect—an uptown city with a down South heart.

Greenville Junior League Publications

Benefactor Acknowledgment

We gratefully acknowledge the financial assistance of the following corporations as it exemplifies not only their support for the purpose of the Junior League of Greenville, Inc., but also their concern for the needs of our community.

Grand Benefactors

Citizens and Southern National Bank
First Union National Bank of South Carolina
NCNB South Carolina

Benefactors

Canal Insurance Company
South Carolina National Bank

Table of Contents

Morning Menus

Midday Menus

Evening Meals

UPTOWN DOWN SOUTH

A Collection Of Preferred Menus

THE JUNIOR LEAGUE OF GREENVILLE, INC.

GREENVILLE, SOUTH CAROLINA

The purpose of the Junior League is to promote voluntarism, to develop the potential of its members for voluntary participation in community affairs and to demonstrate the effectiveness of trained volunteers.

Proceeds from the sale of *Uptown Down South* are returned to the community through volunteer projects of the Junior League of Greenville, Inc.

Copyright 1986
Greenville Junior League Publications
Greenville, South Carolina
All Rights Reserved
ISBN 0-960817212

First printing	10,000 copies	October 1986
Second printing	10,000 copies	December 1986
Third printing	10,000 copies	October 1988
Fourth printing	10,000 copies	December 1990

Copies of *Uptown Down South* may be obtained from

Greenville Junior League Publications
17 West North Street
Greenville, South Carolina 29601
or by mailing order blank at the back of the book.

Printed in the USA by
WIMMER BROTHERS
A Wimmer Company
Memphis • Dallas

MORNING MENUS

MENU: "HONORING THE MOTHER-TO-BE"

Southern Thanksgiving Brunch

Serves 8

Wine Welcomer
Sausage Brunch Casserole
Baked Garlic Cheese Grits
Marinated Cherry Tomatoes
Almond-Curried Fruit
Flaky Light Biscuits
Strawberry Butter
Peach Preserves
Spiced Apple Coffee Cake

Wine Welcomer

2 cups orange juice
6 ounces frozen lemonade, thawed
4 cups dry white wine, chilled
33.8 ounces club soda, chilled
Crushed ice
Orange slices

Stir together orange juice, lemonade and wine in large container. Add club soda just before serving. Serve in wine glasses over crushed ice. Garnish with orange slices. Yield: 10½ cups.

Sausage Brunch Casserole

1½ pounds sausage
1 2½-ounce jar sliced mushrooms
6 slices white bread, crusts removed
2 cups grated cheddar cheese
2½ cups milk
4 large eggs, beaten
¼ teaspoon dry mustard
1 10¾-ounce can cream of mushroom soup
¼ teaspoon grated onion
½ teaspoon Worcestershire sauce
Fresh parsley sprigs, optional

Brown sausage and drain well. Drain mushrooms. Cut bread into cubes. In a very large mixing bowl, combine sausage, mushrooms, bread and remaining ingredients; stir well. Generously butter 9x13x2-inch baking dish. Pour mixture into dish; cover and refrigerate overnight. Bake, uncovered, at 300° for 1½ hours. Garnish with parsley sprigs. Serves 8.

Baked Garlic Cheese Grits

4 cups water
1 cup quick grits
1 teaspoon salt
½ cup butter

1 6-ounce roll garlic cheese
2 large eggs, beaten
½ cup milk

Cook grits in water and salt. When thickened add butter and cheese. Mix thoroughly until melted. Stir in eggs and milk. Pour into greased 11¾x7½x1¾-inch baking dish. Can be refrigerated before baking. Bake at 350° for 45 minutes. Serves 8.

Marinated Cherry Tomatoes

2 teaspoons salt
1 teaspoon sugar
½ teaspoon pepper
1½ cups oil
1 teaspoon paprika

¼ cup white vinegar
¼ cup wine vinegar
⅛ teaspoon garlic salt
2 pints cherry tomatoes, halved

Make marinade by combining all ingredients except tomatoes in covered container. Shake vigorously. Pour over cherry tomatoes. Cover and marinate in refrigerator for several hours. Serves 8.

Almond-Curried Fruit

1 29-ounce can sliced peaches
1 15½-ounce can pineapple
  chunks
1 16-ounce can pear halves
1 6-ounce jar maraschino
  cherries

½ cup slivered almonds, toasted
⅓ cup butter, melted
¾ cup brown sugar, firmly
  packed
1 tablespoon curry powder

Drain all fruits and arrange in 9x13x2-inch baking dish. Sprinkle fruit with almonds. Combine butter, brown sugar and curry powder. Top fruit with brown sugar mixture. Bake at 325° for 1 hour. Serves 8.

Flaky Light Biscuits

¼ cup shortening
2 cups self-rising flour

¾ cup buttermilk

Cut shortening into flour until mixture resembles coarse meal. Add buttermilk and stir well. Turn dough onto floured surface and knead lightly 10-12 times. Add more flour if necessary. Roll dough out to thickness of ¼ inch. Cut with biscuit cutter. Place biscuits on lightly greased baking sheet. Bake at 450° for 10 minutes or until lightly browned. Yield: 24 biscuits.

Strawberry Butter

1 cup butter, softened   ½ cup strawberry jam

Place butter and jam in food processor and process until well blended. Chill. Yield: 1½ cups.

Peach Preserves

1 quart ripe peaches, finely   Juice of ½ lemon
  diced   2 cups sugar

Boil peaches, lemon juice and sugar for 10 minutes. Remove from heat and pour into shallow glass dish. Allow to stand overnight. It is not necessary to refrigerate this mixture. Next day, return mixture to pan and bring back to a boil. Pour into sterilized half pint jars. Cover with paraffin. Yield: 4-5 jars.

Spiced Apple Coffee Cake

2¼ cups plain flour   3 large eggs
  2 cups sugar   2 cups thinly sliced apples
  ½ teaspoon salt   1 cup powdered sugar
  ½ teaspoon baking soda   2 tablespoons milk
  1 teaspoon vanilla extract   1 teaspoon cinnamon
  1 cup butter   ¼ cup finely chopped pecans
  8 ounces spiced apple yogurt

Combine first 8 ingredients in large bowl and blend at low speed. Beat at medium speed for 3 more minutes. Stir in apples. Pour batter into greased Bundt pan. Bake at 325° for 60-65 minutes. Cool 15 minutes before removing from pan. Make glaze by mixing powdered sugar, milk and cinnamon until smooth. Drizzle glaze over warm cake and sprinkle with chopped pecans. Serves 12-16.

This menu works well anytime family or friends gather for the holidays. To carry out the Thanksgiving theme, use a cornucopia filled with the biscuits as your centerpiece. For color add traditional holiday greens and fruits.

Mountain Weekend Hearty Breakfast

Serves 8

Glazed Canadian Bacon
Scrambled Eggs Casserole
Winter Vegetable Salad
Baked Apple Doughnuts
Almond Crusted Torte

Glazed Canadian Bacon

2 pounds Canadian bacon
Whole cloves
¾ cup water
¾ cup red wine

1 12-ounce jar currant jelly
1 tablespoon vinegar
1 teaspoon prepared mustard
½ teaspoon ground cloves

Preheat oven to 350°. Place bacon in baking dish and stud with cloves. Combine water and red wine in saucepan and heat. Pour over bacon. Bake covered for 1½ hours. Make a sauce from remaining ingredients. Baste meat every 10 minutes with sauce during last ½ hour of cooking. Slice thinly and serve warm with remaining sauce. Serves 8.

Scrambled Eggs Casserole

2 tablespoons butter
2½ tablespoons plain flour
2 cups milk
½ teaspoon salt
⅛ teaspoon pepper
8 ounces cream cheese, cubed
¼ cup chopped green onion
3 tablespoons butter, melted

1 dozen eggs, beaten
½ teaspoon salt
¼ teaspoon pepper
1 4-ounce can sliced mushrooms
¼ cup butter
2¼ cups soft bread crumbs
⅛ teaspoon paprika

To prepare cheese sauce, melt 2 tablespoons butter in heavy sauce pan over low heat; blend in flour and cook 1 minute. Gradually add milk; cook over medium heat until thickened, stirring constantly. Add ½ teaspoon salt, ⅛ teaspoon pepper and cream cheese, stirring until cheese melts and mixture is smooth. In large skillet, sauté green onion in 3 tablespoons butter. Add eggs, salt and pepper and cook over medium high heat, stirring to form large, soft curds. Drain mushrooms. When eggs are set, stir in mushrooms and cheese sauce. Spoon eggs into greased 9x13x2-inch baking pan. Combine ¼ cup melted butter and bread crumbs; mix well. Spread buttered crumbs evenly over egg mixture. Sprinkle with paprika. Cover and chill overnight. Uncover and bake at 350° for 30 minutes or until heated thoroughly. Serves 12.

Winter Vegetable Salad

1 large bunch broccoli
1 large head cauliflower
3 medium carrots
10 ounces frozen green peas
¾ cup Dijon-style mustard
¾ cup sour cream

¾ cup mayonnaise
2 teaspoons celery seeds
2 tablespoons dried tarragon
½ cup chopped fresh parsley
Pepper to taste

Cut broccoli and cauliflower into small florets. Slice carrots into ¼-inch rounds. Bring pot of salted water to a boil. Drop broccoli into water and boil for 1 minute. Remove from water and drop immediately into bowl of cold water. Drop cauliflower into boiling water and boil for 2 minutes. Transfer to bowl of cold water. Drop carrots and peas into boiling water and boil for 1 minute. Transfer to bowl of cold water. Drain all vegetables thoroughly and toss in large mixing bowl. In another bowl, whisk remaining ingredients together and pour over vegetables. Toss gently but thoroughly. Cover and chill before serving. Serves 12.

Baked Apple Doughnuts

1½ cups sifted plain flour
1¾ teaspoons baking powder
½ teaspoon salt
½ teaspoon nutmeg
½ cup sugar
⅓ cup shortening

1 egg, beaten
¼ cup milk
½ cup peeled and grated apple
⅓ cup sugar
1 teaspoon cinnamon
½ cup butter, melted

Sift together flour, baking powder, salt, nutmeg and ½ cup sugar. Cut in shortening until mixture is fine. Mix together egg, milk and apple. Add all at once to dry ingredients and mix quickly but thoroughly. Fill greased muffin pans ⅔ full. Bake at 350° for 20-25 minutes or until golden brown. Combine cinnamon and sugar in bowl. Remove doughnuts from pan; cool slightly. Roll in melted butter and then in cinnamon and sugar mixture. Yield: 1 dozen.

Almond Crusted Torte

1⅔ cups plain flour
1½ cups sugar
1 cup butter, melted
⅛ teaspoon salt

2 tablespoons almond extract
2 eggs, beaten
No-stick vegetable spray
2¼ ounces sliced almonds

Stir together all ingredients except almonds. Pour into 10-inch pie pan that has been sprayed with no-stick vegetable product. Sprinkle almonds over top. Bake at 350° for 35-40 minutes or until lightly browned. Serves 8.

The Children's Favorite Breakfast

Serves 4

Triple Fruit Icee
Strawberry Glazed Grapefruit
Rise and Shine Waffles
Sour Cream Blueberry Pancakes
Breakfast Ovencake
Cinnamon-Honey Syrup

Triple Fruit Icee

6 ounces frozen lemonade
6 ounces frozen limeade
6 ounces frozen pineapple juice

4 cups cold water
Crushed ice
Lemon slices

Combine frozen concentrates in pitcher. Thaw partially, then stir until smooth. Gradually stir in cold water. Add crushed ice and garnish with lemon slices. May substitute 1 quart of chilled ginger ale for water. Yield: 10 4-ounce servings.

Strawberry Glazed Grapefruit

4 large grapefruit
1 pint strawberries

¼ cup orange juice
½ cup sugar

Cut grapefruit in half; seed, section and refrigerate. Wash and cap strawberries and combine with sugar and orange juice. Heat for 3 minutes, stirring constantly. Refrigerate and serve over grapefruit. Serves 8.

Rise and Shine Waffles

1½ cups whole wheat flour
2 teaspoons baking powder
½ teaspoon salt
2 cups milk
2 eggs

¼ cup butter, melted
3 tablespoons honey
1 cup rolled oats, uncooked
1 cup finely chopped nuts

Combine flour, baking powder and salt. Add milk, eggs, butter and honey; mix until smooth. Stir in oats and nuts. Cook in oiled waffle iron about 4-5 minutes or until lightly browned. Yield: 6 8-inch waffles.

Sour Cream Blueberry Pancakes

2 cups milk
2 eggs
½ cup sour cream
2 cups plain flour
2 tablespoons baking powder

2 tablespoons sugar
½ teaspoon salt
4 tablespoons butter, melted
1 cup fresh blueberries

Combine milk, eggs and sour cream and beat well. Stir together flour, baking powder, sugar and salt. Add to egg mixture. Beat just until large lumps disappear. Stir in butter. Fold in blueberries. Pour about ¼ cup batter on hot, lightly greased griddle for each pancake. When edges begin to look dry, turn pancakes and watch carefully. Can be frozen after pancakes have cooled on wire rack. Drizzle lightly with syrup. Yield: 18 4-inch pancakes.

Breakfast Ovencake

4 tablespoons butter
½ cup plain flour
½ cup milk

2 eggs, beaten
2 tablespoons powdered sugar

Melt butter in an 8-inch or 10-inch iron skillet in 425° oven. While butter is melting, mix together flour, milk and eggs. Mix to blend ingredients. When butter has melted, pour flour mixture into hot skillet and bake in oven for 15-20 minutes. Remove from oven and sprinkle with powdered sugar. Cut into wedges. Serve with syrup or jelly. Serves 4.

Cinnamon-Honey Syrup

½ cup brown sugar, firmly
   packed
1½ cups sugar
1 cup water

1 cup honey
1½ teaspoons cinnamon
½ teaspoon maple flavoring

Combine brown sugar, sugar and water in saucepan. Bring mixture to boil; remove from heat. Stir in remaining ingredients. Yield: 2¾ cups.

Breakfast will be a special time for your children when you let them choose the waffles, pancakes or ovencake. The children can do their part by mixing the Triple Fruit Icee.

Drop-in Brunch for Holiday Shoppers

Serves 8

Ham and Broccoli Strata
Divine Carrots and Apples
Cranberry Cream
Whole Wheat Popovers
Lemon Heaven
Cinnamon Laced Coffee

Ham and Broccoli Strata

10 ounces frozen chopped
   broccoli
10 slices white bread
2 cups diced cooked ham
6 eggs, slightly beaten
3½ cups milk
1 tablespoon instant minced
   onion

¼ teaspoon dry mustard
3 cups shredded sharp cheddar
   cheese
Fresh parsley sprigs, optional
Hard-cooked egg slices,
   optional
Paprika, optional

Cook broccoli according to package directions; drain. Remove crusts from bread and cut into small cubes. Layer bread cubes, broccoli and ham in buttered 11¾x7½x1¾-inch baking dish. Combine beaten eggs, milk, onion, mustard, and cheese; stir well. Pour over casserole. Cover and refrigerate 24 hours. Bake uncovered at 325° for 55-60 minutes. Garnish with parsley, egg slices and paprika, if desired. Serves 8.

Divine Carrots and Apples

8 medium carrots
12 medium cooking apples
¾ cup butter

1½ cups sugar
¼ cup water

Peel carrots and slice. Cook in boiling water for 20 minutes or until tender. Drain well. Peel and core apples and slice into large pieces. In 2-quart baking dish, layer ⅓ of apples and then ⅓ of carrots. Dot with butter and sprinkle liberally with sugar. Repeat until all ingredients are used. Add water. Bake in 350° oven for 30 minutes or until apples are tender. Serves 8.

Cranberry Cream

8 ounces cream cheese, softened
½ cup whole cranberry sauce

Combine ingredients in blender or food processor and blend until smooth. Serve with whole wheat popovers. Yield: 1 cup.

16

Whole Wheat Popovers

2 large eggs, beaten
1 cup milk
1 tablespoon butter, melted

⅔ cup whole wheat flour
⅓ cup plain flour
¼ teaspoon salt

Put all ingredients in bowl and mix without overbeating. Half fill buttered muffin tins. Place in cold oven; bake at 450° for 15 minutes. Reduce heat to 350°; bake additional 10-15 minutes. Serve immediately. Yield: 1 dozen.

Lemon Heaven

1 cup plain flour
½ cup butter
1 cup chopped nuts
8 ounces cream cheese, softened
9 ounces refrigerated non-dairy topping, divided

½ cup powdered sugar
2 3½-ounce packages instant lemon pudding
3 cups cold milk

In mixing bowl, cut butter into flour until crumbly; stir in nuts. Press mixture into greased 9x13x2-inch baking pan. Bake at 325° for 20-25 minutes. Cool crust completely. Whip together cream cheese, 1 cup non-dairy topping and powdered sugar until smooth; spread over cooled crust. Combine pudding mix with milk and spread over cream cheese layer. Ice with remaining non-dairy topping and chill 2 hours. Serves 12.

Cinnamon Laced Coffee

2 sticks cinnamon or ¼ teaspoon ground cinnamon
1 pound coffee

Follow manufacturer's instructions to brew 10 cups of coffee. Combine cinnamon sticks or ground cinnamon and coffee grounds in basket of coffee maker. Brew coffee as directed. Yield: 10 cups.

A thriving "uptown" district, plus an abundance of shopping malls, antique shops, boutiques and outlet malls make Greenville a popular shopping place throughout the year. During the holidays this delightful brunch is the perfect way to share the Christmas spirit with friends as they finish their shopping for everything on Santa's lists.

Honoring the Mother to Be

Serves 12

Sherry Slush Appetizer
Icebox Cheese Wafers
Baked Toast Amaretto
Maple Almond Syrup
Orange Mousse
Frosted Grapes

Sherry Slush Appetizer

1 6-ounce can frozen orange juice
1 6-ounce can frozen lemonade
1 6-ounce can frozen limeade
½ quart ginger ale
Sherry
12 small wine glasses
12 small stirring straws

Thaw orange juice, lemonade and limeade concentrates. Stir in ginger ale and freeze overnight. When ready to serve, scoop a mound of slush mixture into each wine glass. Add sherry to taste. Serve immediately with small stirring straws. Serves 12.

Icebox Cheese Wafers

½ cup butter, softened
2 cups grated sharp cheddar cheese
1 cup plain flour
¼ teaspoon red pepper
1 teaspoon salt
¾ cup finely chopped pecans

Cream butter. Add remaining ingredients and work together with hands. Shape mixture into roll, approximately 1½ inches in diameter; wrap in plastic wrap. Freeze overnight. When ready to serve, remove roll from freezer and let stand for 5 minutes. Slice thinly and place on cookie sheet. Bake at 375° for 10 minutes. These wafers are delicious either warm or at room temperature. Yield: 54 wafers.

Baked Toast Amaretto

½ cup butter, melted and divided
7 eggs, beaten
½ cup milk
¼ cup sugar
2 tablespoons Amaretto
1 16-ounce loaf French bread

Divide ¼ cup melted butter into two 15x10x1-inch jelly roll pans; spread evenly and set aside. Combine remaining ¼ cup butter, eggs, milk, sugar and Amaretto in large mixing bowl. Cut bread into ¾-inch slices. Dip slices of bread, 1 at a time, into egg mixture, coating well. Arrange in single layer in prepared pans. Bake at 450° for 20 minutes, turning once, until golden. Serve with Maple Almond Syrup. Serves 10-12.

Maple Almond Syrup

2 tablespoons butter
½ cup sliced almonds

1½ cups maple syrup
¼ cup Amaretto

Melt butter in small saucepan; add almonds and sauté over medium heat until golden. Stir in maple syrup and Amaretto. Serve warm over baked toast. Yield: 1⅔ cups.

Orange Mousse

2 envelopes unflavored gelatin
1½ cups sugar
⅛ teaspoon salt
4 egg yolks
2½ cups orange juice, divided

3 tablespoons lemon juice
1 tablespoon grated orange rind
2 11-ounce cans mandarin oranges
2 cups whipping cream, whipped

Thoroughly mix gelatin, sugar and salt in saucepan. Beat together egg yolks and 1 cup orange juice. Stir into gelatin mixture and cook over medium heat, stirring constantly until mixture comes to a boil. Remove from heat and stir in remaining juices and orange rind. Chill, stirring occasionally until mixture mounds when dropped from spoon. Stir in drained mandarin oranges and fold in whipped cream. Pour into large ring mold and chill. Unmold onto serving platter and garnish with frosted grapes. Serves 12.

Frosted Grapes

1 large bunch green or red grapes

2 egg whites, slightly beaten
1 cup sugar

Wash and dry grapes thoroughly. Break into small clusters. Dip each cluster into slightly beaten egg whites. Toss each cluster in bag with granulated sugar. Place sugar-coated grapes on towel to dry. Arrange around mousse on platter. May also frost entire bunch of grapes as described above and arrange on platter with ivy or galax as a pretty addition to any table.

Entertain the mother to be in an elegant fashion. Arrange baked toast on large silver serving tray and surround with link sausage and bacon. Use spiced apple rings or strawberries for garnish. Serve warm syrup from a small silver pitcher or gravy boat with ladle.

Furman Kickoff Brunch

Serves 12

Ham and Spinach Rolls
Cheddar Cheese Puff
Cranberry-Apple Crunch
Extra Special Biscuits
Sweet Potato Cake

Ham and Spinach Rolls

2 10½-ounce cans cream of
   celery soup
1 cup sour cream
3 tablespoons Dijon-style
   mustard
2 10-ounce packages frozen
   spinach
1½ cups cooked rice

2 cups cottage cheese
3 eggs, slightly beaten
¾ cup finely chopped onion
6 tablespoons plain flour
24 thin slices of boiled ham
   Dried bread crumbs
   Fresh parsley, chopped
   Paprika

In small bowl, combine soup, sour cream and mustard; mix well. Thaw frozen chopped spinach and drain. In large bowl, combine spinach, rice, cottage cheese, eggs, onion and flour; mix well. Add ½ cup of soup mixture to rice and spinach mixture; mix well. Place 2 tablespoons of mixture on each slice of ham. Roll ham slices and secure with toothpicks. Arrange in 2 rows of 6 each, seam side down in two 11¾x7½x1¾-inch greased baking dishes. Top ham rolls with remaining soup mixture. Sprinkle bread crumbs, parsley and paprika on top. Bake at 350° for 35 minutes. Serves 12.

Cheddar Cheese Puff

4 eggs
4 tablespoons plain flour
2 cups milk
1 pound sharp cheddar cheese,
   grated

20 Ritz crackers, crushed
¼ cup butter

In double boiler combine eggs, flour and milk. Cook, stirring constantly until thick. Mixture will appear lumpy. Remove from heat. Place ½ of grated cheese in greased 2-quart round baking dish. Pour ½ egg mixture over cheese. Layer remaining cheese. Pour remaining egg mixture over cheese layer. Top with cracker crumbs. Dot with butter. Bake at 350° for 30 minutes. Prepare recipe twice to serve 12. Serves 6.

Cranberry-Apple Crunch

6 cups peeled and chopped
  cooking apples
2 16-ounce cans whole
  cranberry sauce
2 cups rolled oats, uncooked

1 cup brown sugar, firmly
  packed
2 cups chopped pecans
1 cup butter, melted

In two 2-quart buttered casseroles, layer apples and cranberry sauce. Combine oats, brown sugar and nuts; mix until crumbly. Sprinkle crumb mixture over fruit. Pour melted butter over top. Bake at 350° for 30 minutes or until apples are tender. Serves 12.

Extra Special Biscuits

2 cups plain flour
¾ cup cornmeal
1 tablespoon baking powder
1 teaspoon salt

½ teaspoon baking soda
1 tablespoon sugar
½ cup butter, softened
1 cup buttermilk

Combine dry ingredients and mix well. Cut in butter until mixture resembles coarse meal. Add buttermilk, stirring until dry ingredients are moistened. Turn dough onto floured surface and knead several times. Roll dough to ½-inch thickness and cut with 2-inch biscuit cutter. Place biscuits on lightly greased baking sheet. Bake at 450° for 10-12 minutes. Yield: 2 dozen.

Sweet Potato Cake

1 cup butter
2 cups sugar
4 eggs
2½ cups mashed sweet potatoes
3 cups plain flour
2 teaspoons baking powder
½ teaspoon salt

1 teaspoon baking soda
1 teaspoon cinnamon
½ teaspoon nutmeg
½ cup chopped nuts
½ cup flaked coconut
1 teaspoon vanilla extract

In large mixing bowl, cream butter and sugar. Add eggs one at a time, beating well after each addition. Mix in sweet potatoes. Sift together flour, baking powder, salt, baking soda, cinnamon and nutmeg. Gradually add flour mixture to butter mixture, beating well. Stir in nuts, coconut and vanilla. Pour into greased and floured 12-cup Bundt pan. Bake at 325° for 1¼ hours. Yield: 24 slices.

Football fans can delight in spending crisp fall afternoons on the lovely Furman University campus cheering for the Paladins. With the campus and stadium only a few minutes drive from downtown Greenville, pre-game brunches are a favorite warm-up for football fans, home team and visitors, alike!

Christmas Cookie Swap

Serves 6

Molasses Sugar Cookies
Chocolate Mint Rounds
One-Is-Enough Cookies
Jumbo Cartwheels
Christmas Cookies
Scotch Shortbread Squares
Chocolate Winter Warm-Up
Holiday Spirit Spritzer

Molasses Sugar Cookies

¾ cup shortening
1 cup sugar
¼ cup molasses
1 egg
2 cups plain flour, sifted
2 teaspoons baking soda
¼ teaspoon ground cloves
¼ teaspoon ground ginger
1 teaspoon ground cinnamon
½ teaspoon salt
Granulated sugar

Melt shortening in saucepan over low heat; cool. Add sugar, molasses, and egg; beat well. Sift together flour, soda, cloves, ginger, cinnamon and salt; add to first mixture. Mix well and chill. Form into 1-inch balls; roll in granulated sugar and place on greased cookie sheet. Bake at 375° for 8-10 minutes. Yield: 4 dozen.

Chocolate Mint Rounds

4 ounces unsweetened chocolate
1¼ cups shortening
2 cups sugar
2 eggs
⅓ cup light corn syrup
2½ tablespoons water
2 teaspoons peppermint extract
1 teaspoon vanilla extract
4 cups plain flour
2 teaspoons baking soda
½ teaspoon salt
Granulated sugar

Melt chocolate over hot water in top of double boiler. Remove from heat. In separate bowl cream shortening; gradually add sugar, beating until light and fluffy. Add melted chocolate, eggs, corn syrup, water and flavorings; mix well. Combine flour, soda and salt; add to creamed mixture, beating just until blended. Shape dough into 1-inch balls and roll in sugar. Place on ungreased cookie sheet. Bake at 350° for 10 minutes. Yield: 10 dozen.

One-Is-Enough Cookies

½ cup butter, softened
1 cup sugar
1½ cups brown sugar, firmly
    packed
3 eggs
1½ cups peanut butter
¼ teaspoon vanilla extract

¾ teaspoon light corn syrup
4½ cups rolled oats, uncooked
2 teaspoons baking soda
¼ teaspoon salt
1 cup M & M plain candies
6 ounces semi-sweet chocolate
    chips

Cream butter and sugars. Add eggs, peanut butter, vanilla and corn syrup; beat well. Add oats, soda, salt; stir well. Stir in remaining ingredients. Drop dough by ¼-cup measures at 4-inch intervals on lightly greased cookie sheet. Bake at 350° for 12-15 minutes. Yield: 2½ dozen.

Jumbo Cartwheels

2 cups plain flour
2 teaspoons baking powder
¾ teaspoon soda
1 teaspoon salt
1 cup butter, softened
2 cups brown sugar, firmly
    packed
2 eggs

1 tablespoon water
1½ teaspoon grated orange rind
1½ cups granola
6 ounces semi-sweet chocolate
    chips
½ cup chopped pecans or
    walnuts

Combine flour, baking powder, soda, and salt; set aside. Cream butter and sugar. Add eggs; beat well. Blend in water and orange rind. Add flour mixture; mix well. Stir in granola, chocolate chips and nuts. Drop by tablespoonfuls onto lightly greased cookie sheet. Bake at 350° for 12 minutes. Yield: 2 dozen.

Christmas Cookies

1 cup shortening
2 cups brown sugar, firmly
    packed
4 cups plain flour
1 teaspoon baking soda
1 teaspoon salt
⅔ cup buttermilk
2 eggs

1 tablespoon rum or brandy
    extract
3 tablespoons grated lemon rind
1 cup red and green candied
    cherries
2 cups chopped dates
1 cup chopped pecans

Cream shortening and sugar; set aside. In separate bowl, mix flour, soda and salt. Add flour mixture alternately with buttermilk to sugar mixture. Add eggs 1 at a time, beating after each addition. Stir in extract, rind, fruits and nuts. Chill for 3 hours. Drop by teaspoonfuls onto greased cookie sheet at 2-inch intervals. Bake at 375° for 8-10 minutes. Yield: 5 dozen.

Scotch Shortbread Squares

1 cup butter
1 cup powdered sugar

½ cup cornstarch
2½ cups plain flour

Cream butter. Add sugar and cream again. Add cornstarch all at once. Mix well. Add flour gradually, mixing well after each addition. If mixture becomes difficult to work with, mix remaining flour in by hand. Roll out on lightly floured surface and cut into squares. Place squares on cookie sheet and bake at 325° for 20-25 minutes. Yield: 3-4 dozen.

Chocolate Winter Warm-Up

4 ounces unsweetened chocolate
½ cup boiling water
4 cups milk, scalded
2 cups cream
6 tablespoons sugar
¼ teaspoon salt
Pinch of nutmeg

Pinch of allspice
2 teaspoons cinnamon
2 eggs
2 teaspoons vanilla extract
Whipping cream, whipped
Cinnamon

Grate chocolate; heat in top of double boiler. Add boiling water and stir with wooden spoon until chocolate melts; beat until smooth. Stir in hot milk, cream, sugar, salt and spices. Simmer 1 hour, beating vigorously every 10 minutes. When ready to serve, beat eggs with vanilla. Add small amount of hot chocolate to eggs; stir this mixture into remaining chocolate. Beat vigorously 3 minutes. Serve at once in preheated cups or mugs, preferably earthenware. Serve chocolate topped with whipped cream and sprinkled with cinnamon. Serves 8.

Holiday Spirit Spritzer

1 quart apple cider
1 quart ginger ale
12 ounces frozen orange juice

4 cups dry white wine
Orange slices

Combine all ingredients and stir well. Serve over ice and garnish with orange slices. Yield: 12 cups.

A cookie swap is a fun and easy way to entertain for the holidays. Guests are asked to bring seven dozen cookies and copies of their recipe for other guests. A dozen cookies from each recipe are arranged on the table for sampling. Every guest then takes home a dozen cookies from each recipe. The holiday theme can be carried out by serving the cookies in baskets lined with Christmas napkins. For a centerpiece decorate a small tree with ribbon-tied cookie cutters.

Wedding Day Brunch

Serves 40

Champagne Turkey in Toast Cups
Ambrosia Laced Peaches
Peas with Water Chestnuts
Spiced Ginger Muffins
Lemon Sours
Chocolate Cream Bars
Iced Pecan Riches

Champagne Turkey in Toast Cups

22 pound turkey	5 cups evaporated milk
1 medium onion	9 cups turkey broth
1 stalk celery	1 cup butter
1 carrot	3 pounds mushrooms, sliced
1 tablespoon salt	4 cups dry champagne
1½ teaspoons pepper	4 tablespoons dried parsley
2 cups plain flour	40 whole wheat bread slices
4 cups half-and-half	Butter, melted

Place turkey in large Dutch oven; cover with water. Add onion, celery, carrot, salt and pepper. Bring to boil; reduce heat to low and simmer 3-4 hours or until fork tender. Cool turkey; remove skin and bones. Cut turkey into 1-inch cubes. In 10-12 quart pot, blend flour with 3 cups of half-and-half. Gradually stir in remaining half-and-half, evaporated milk and turkey broth. Cook, stirring constantly, until mixture boils. Reduce heat and cook until sauce thickens. In large skillet, melt butter and sauté mushrooms until tender. Stir turkey, mushrooms, champagne, and parsley into cream sauce. Heat through. To make toast cups, brush one side of each slice of bread with butter. With butter side down, bring 4 corners of bread together and place in ungreased muffin pans. Bake at 350° for 10 minutes. Toast cups can be prepared ahead and stored in airtight container. To serve, place turkey in silver chafing dish on silver tray and arrange toast cups around base of chafing dish. Serves 40.

Ambrosia Laced Peaches

1½ cups seedless green grapes
3 15¼-ounce cans pineapple
  tidbits
1½ cups orange sections
1½ cups flaked coconut

1½ cups sour cream
40 peach halves, drained
40 lettuce leaves
1½ cups slivered almonds, toasted

Wash and halve grapes. Drain pineapple tidbits. In bowl, combine grapes, pineapple, oranges and coconut; toss gently and chill. Before serving add sour cream and mix well. Place peach half on lettuce leaf and fill with ¼ cup fruit mixture. Top with almonds. Serves 40.

Peas with Water Chestnuts

5 bacon slices
5 1-pound packages frozen green
  peas

5 8-ounce cans water chestnuts
  Salt and pepper to taste

In large pot fry bacon until crisp; crumble. To bacon drippings add frozen peas and cook according to package directions. Sliver water chestnuts; add to cooked peas along with bacon, salt and pepper. Heat through. Serves 40.

Spiced Ginger Muffins

1 teaspoon baking soda
1 tablespoon hot water
1 cup butter
1 cup sugar
4 egg yolks
1 cup molasses
1 teaspoon nutmeg
1 teaspoon cinnamon

1 teaspoon ginger
3½ cups plain flour
1 cup buttermilk
½ cup raisins, dusted with flour
1 cup chopped nuts
4 egg whites, beaten
  Pinch of salt

Dissolve soda in hot water. Cream butter and sugar in mixing bowl. Add egg yolks, molasses, soda, water, nutmeg, cinnamon and ginger. Add flour alternately with buttermilk. Add raisins and nuts. Beat egg whites with salt until frothy and fold into batter. Grease miniature muffin tins and fill ¾ full with batter. Bake 20 minutes at 350°. May be made ahead and frozen. Serve hot or cold. Yield: 60 miniature muffins.

Lemon Sours

1 cup butter, softened
2 cups plain flour
½ cup powdered sugar
4 eggs
2 cups sugar

6 tablespoons lemon juice
1 tablespoon plain flour
½ teaspoon baking powder
Powdered sugar

Mix together butter, flour and powdered sugar. Press mixture into ungreased 9x13-inch baking pan. Bake at 325° for 15 minutes. In bowl beat eggs, sugar, lemon juice, flour and baking powder. Pour over cooked pastry. Bake at 350° for 40-50 minutes. Let cool and sprinkle with powdered sugar. Cut into 1½-inch squares. Yield: 48 squares.

Chocolate Cream Bars

1 packaged chocolate cake mix
½ cup butter, softened
1 egg
8 ounces cream cheese, softened

1 pound powdered sugar
3 eggs
1 cup finely slivered pecans

Mix together cake mix, butter and egg. Using palm of hand, spread dough into ungreased 10x15-inch jelly roll pan. Mix cream cheese with powdered sugar and eggs. Pour mixture over uncooked chocolate base. Sprinkle top with pecans. Bake at 325° for 30-40 minutes. Place in freezer for 20 minutes. Remove from freezer. Dip knife in hot water and cut dessert into 1x2½-inch bars. Yield: 60 bars.

Iced Pecan Riches

1 cup plain flour
2 tablespoons sugar
½ cup butter, softened
3 eggs
1½ cups brown sugar, firmly packed
2 tablespoons plain flour

1 teaspoon baking powder
1 cup chopped pecans
½ cup flaked coconut
1 teaspoon vanilla extract
2 tablespoons butter, melted
1½ cups powdered sugar
2 tablespoons evaporated milk

In bowl sift 1 cup flour and 2 tablespoons sugar. Blend in butter with hands until dough is smooth. Pat into greased 9-inch square pan. Bake at 325° for 10-15 minutes. Meanwhile, beat together eggs, brown sugar, flour and baking powder. Stir in pecans, coconut and vanilla. Pour over baked crust and bake 25 minutes. To prepare frosting combine melted butter, powdered sugar and milk. Spread over cooled pan mixture. Cut into 1½-inch squares. Yield: 36 squares.

Couple's Weekend Brunch

Serves 8

Eye-Opener Tomato Cocktail
Cheddar Egg Bake
Sausage and Apple Rings
Orange Zested Grits
Blueberry Crumb Muffins

Eye-Opener Tomato Cocktail

1 46-ounce can tomato juice
2 teaspoons Worcestershire
   sauce
2 tablespoons lime juice
1 teaspoon onion juice
6 drops hot sauce
1 teaspoon celery seeds

Combine all ingredients in large pitcher; mix well. Chill until ready to serve. Yield: 1½ quarts.

Cheddar Egg Bake

2½ cups shredded sharp cheddar
    cheese
12 eggs
1½ cups sour cream
⅔ cup milk
2 tablespoons plain flour
2 teaspoons prepared mustard
1 teaspoon dried chives
1 teaspoon seasoned salt
2 teaspoons Worcestershire
   sauce
1½ teaspoons pepper
6 English muffins, split
   Fresh parsley sprigs
   Paprika

Sprinkle ½ of cheese evenly over bottom of greased 9x13x2-inch casserole. Break eggs and slip onto cheese in dish. Beat together sour cream, milk, flour, mustard, chives, salt, Worcestershire sauce and pepper. Pour over eggs. Sprinkle evenly with remaining cheese. Bake at 325° for 25-30 minutes, until whites are set and yolks are soft and creamy. To serve, place 1 egg on each muffin half. Spoon sauce over each serving. Garnish with fresh parsley and paprika. Serves 8.

Sausage and Apple Rings

24 ounces bulk pork sausage
4 large cooking apples, cored
⅔ cup sugar
1 teaspoon cinnamon
4 tablespoons butter
¼ cup chopped fresh parsley

Shape pork sausage into ¼-inch thick patties, 3½ inches in diameter. In 12-inch skillet, cook sausage patties over medium heat until well browned on both sides, about 10-15 minutes. Drain well. Keep warm. Wipe skillet clean. Slice ends off unpeeled apples; cut each into 3 slices. Combine sugar and cinnamon in flat dish. Dip apple slices into mixture and coat both sides. In skillet, over medium high heat, melt butter. Add apple slices, a few at a time, and sauté until golden brown on both sides. Turn apples frequently and sprinkle lightly with some of the remaining sugar mixture. Remove to serving platter and top each ring with sausage. Serve warm, garnished with parsley. Serves 8.

Orange Zested Grits

3 cups water
1 teaspoon salt
1 cup uncooked quick-cooking grits
¼ cup butter
1 teaspoon grated orange rind
1 cup orange juice
4 eggs, beaten
2 tablespoons brown sugar

Bring water and salt to a boil; add grits. Cook over medium heat for 3 minutes, stirring constantly. Remove from heat; add butter, orange rind, orange juice, and eggs. Mix well. Pour mixture into greased 1½-quart baking dish. Sprinkle with brown sugar. Bake at 350° for 45 minutes or until knife inserted in center comes out clean. Serves 8.

Blueberry Crumb Muffins

⅓ cup sugar
¼ cup butter, softened
1 egg
2⅓ cups plain flour
4 teaspoons baking powder
½ teaspoon salt
1 cup milk
1 teaspoon vanilla extract
1½ cups fresh blueberries
½ cup sugar
⅓ cup plain flour
½ teaspoon cinnamon
¼ cup butter, softened

Combine first 2 ingredients, creaming until light and fluffy. Add egg, beating well. Sift together 2⅓ cups flour, baking powder and salt; add to cream mixture alternately with milk. Stir in vanilla and blueberries. Fill greased muffin cups ⅔ full with batter. Combine ½ cup sugar, ⅓ cup flour and cinnamon. Cut in ¼ cup butter until mixture resembles coarse meal. Sprinkle on top of muffins and bake at 375° for 25-30 minutes or until golden brown. Yield: 18 muffins.

Traditional Southern Coffee

Serves 40

Asparagus Vegetable Rolls
Peach Bread Sandwiches
Black-Eyed Susans
Lemon-Raisin Spread
Honey Bars
Amaretto Pound Cake
Coffee Frappé
Pineapple-Orange Tea

Asparagus Vegetable Rolls

3 4-ounce jars chopped
pimentos
3 large bell peppers, finely
chopped
3 teaspoons paprika
3 tablespoons grated onion

Salt to taste
Mayonnaise
3 loaves bread
3 6-ounce cans asparagus spears
½ cup butter, melted
Paprika

Drain pimentos. Mix first 5 ingredients with enough mayonnaise to spread.
Trim crust from bread; roll bread flat. Spread each slice with vegetable
mixture. Place asparagus spear on each slice of bread and roll up tightly.
Place seam side down on baking sheet. Brush rolls liberally with melted
butter. Sprinkle with paprika. When ready to serve, broil until golden.
Yield: 60-66 rolls.

Peach Bread Sandwiches

4 cups unsifted plain flour
4 teaspoons baking powder
1 teaspoon salt
1 teaspoon nutmeg
1 cup butter, softened
1½ cups light corn syrup
½ cup sugar

2 eggs
2 cups puréed peaches
2 cups chopped pecans
8 ounces cream cheese,
softened
1 cup peach preserves

To prepare bread, stir together flour, baking powder, salt and nutmeg;
set aside. Beat butter until smooth. Add corn syrup and sugar; beat until
smooth. Add eggs and beat 1-2 minutes. Add flour mixture alternately with
peaches. Stir in pecans. Bake at 375° for 60-65 minutes in two 9x5x3-inch
greased loaf pans. Cool 10 minutes in pan. Remove from pan and cool on
wire rack. Wrap loaf in foil. Bread is best when made day before. To prepare
sandwich filling, blend cream cheese and peach preserves. Cut loaves into
½-inch slices. Prepare sandwiches and cut each into 3 finger sandwiches.
Yield: 54 finger sandwiches.

Black-Eyed Susans

1 cup butter, softened
1 pound sharp cheddar cheese, grated
3 cups plain flour, sifted
1 teaspoon salt
½ teaspoon red pepper
1 pound whole dates, pitted
Pecan halves
Powdered sugar

Mix butter, cheese, flour, salt and pepper. Shape dough into ball and chill. While dough is chilling, stuff each date with pecan half. Divide chilled dough and roll out onto lightly floured surface. Using 2-inch cookie cutter, cut dough. Put stuffed date in center of each pastry round. Fold dough over to the center from 2 sides and press together. The other 2 ends will remain open. Bake at 325° for 12-15 minutes or until lightly browned. When cool, sprinkle with powdered sugar. Yield: 6 dozen.

Lemon-Raisin Spread

1 cup sugar
½ cup butter
1 egg
Juice of 2 lemons
1 teaspoon grated lemon rind
1 cup mayonnaise
1 cup chopped pecans
1 cup chopped raisins
Ritz crackers

In saucepan mix together sugar, butter, egg, lemon juice and lemon rind; cook until thickened. Remove from heat and stir in mayonnaise, pecans and raisins. Chill. Serve in crystal or silver bowl with Ritz crackers. Yield: 3 cups.

Honey Bars

¾ cup oil
¼ cup honey
1 cup sugar
2 cups plain flour
1½ teaspoons cinnamon
½ teaspoon salt
1 teaspoon baking soda
1 egg
1 cup chopped pecans
1 cup powdered sugar
2 tablespoons mayonnaise
1 tablespoon water
1 teaspoon vanilla extract

Preheat oven to 300°. Blend first 8 ingredients. Stir in chopped nuts. Bake in greased 9x13-inch baking pan for 25-30 minutes. To prepare glaze, combine remaining ingredients. Spread glaze over honey bars while hot. Yield: 54 1x2¼-inch bars.

Amaretto Pound Cake

1 yellow cake mix with pudding
¼ cup oil
3 tablespoons butter
¾ cup Amaretto

4 eggs, room temperature
4 tablespoons butter, melted
1 tablespoon Amaretto
1 cup powdered sugar

In a very large bowl, blend first 4 ingredients for 4 minutes at medium speed. Add eggs 1 at a time, beating 1 minute after each addition. Bake in greased and floured Bundt pan at 325° for 1 hour. To prepare glaze, combine remaining ingredients. Spread glaze over slightly warm cake. Yield: 24 slices.

Coffee Frappé

3 quarts water
¾ cup instant coffee granules
1 cup sugar

2½ gallons vanilla ice cream
1 cup whipping cream
Nutmeg, optional

Day before serving, prepare mold of triple strength coffee. To prepare mold, dissolve 4 tablespoons of coffee granules in 1 quart of boiling water. Pour into mold and freeze. Day of serving, dissolve 8 tablespoons of coffee granules in 2 quarts boiling water. Add 1 cup sugar, stirring to dissolve. Refrigerate until ready to prepare punch bowl. One half hour before serving, remove ice cream from freezer. Pour coffee into large punch bowl. Add mold. Do not put mold in first, as bowl may crack. Mash softened ice cream; add to coffee. Pour whipping cream over top. Sprinkle with nutmeg, if desired. Yield: 50 servings.

Pineapple-Orange Tea

1 gallon water
8 tea bags
2½ cups sugar
2 cups water

2 tablespoons whole cloves
1 46-ounce can pineapple juice
1 46-ounce can orange juice

Place 1 gallon of water in large pot and bring to a boil. Add tea bags. Remove from heat and let steep for 3 minutes. In saucepan, combine sugar with 2 cups water and bring to a boil. Add cloves and boil for 10 minutes, stirring often until syrupy. Add syrup to steeped tea. Mix in juices. Strain to remove cloves. Refrigerate at least 4 hours, preferably overnight. Tea can be refrigerated for 2-3 weeks and prepared as desired. Serve either hot or cold. Yield: 2 gallons.

Welcome to the Neighborhood Coffee

Serves 25

Golden Sausage Nuggets
Rum Cake
Caramel Nut Ring
Cream Cheese Danish
Fresh Fruit with Ginger Crème
Vegetable-Ham Tartlets
Moravian Coffee
Chilled Mint Tea

Golden Sausage Nuggets

1 pound hot bulk pork sausage
¾ cup dry bread crumbs
⅓ cup chicken broth
⅛ teaspoon nutmeg
¼ teaspoon poultry seasoning
1½ cups plain flour
¼ teaspoon salt
1 teaspoon paprika
2 cups shredded sharp cheddar cheese
½ cup butter, softened

Combine first 5 ingredients; mix well. Shape into 1-inch balls. Cook over low heat until done, turning to brown on all sides. Drain on paper towels. Combine flour, salt, paprika, and cheese. Cut in butter with pastry blender. Mix with hands until dough is smooth. Shape 1 tablespoon of dough around each sausage ball, covering sausage completely. Sausage balls may be frozen. Thaw before baking. Place on greased baking sheets. Bake at 350° for 15-20 minutes. Yield: 4 dozen.

Rum Cake

1 cup butter, softened
1½ cups sugar
4 eggs yolks
1½ cups cake flour, sifted
1¼ teaspoons baking powder
1 teaspoon vanilla extract
1 teaspoon almond extract
4 tablespoons rum
4 egg whites, stiffly beaten
½ cup crushed pecans
Pinch of salt

Preheat oven to 325°. Cream butter and sugar. Add egg yolks, 1 at a time, beating well. Sift flour with baking powder. Combine flavorings. Add flour and flavorings alternately. Fold in stiffly beaten egg whites. Grease tube pan and line bottom with waxed paper. Toss pecans with salt and cover bottom of pan. Spoon in batter. Bake at 325° for 1 hour. Cool in pan 10-15 minutes before turning out. Serves 16-20.

Caramel Nut Ring

½ cup butter
½ cup chopped pecans
1 cup brown sugar, firmly
 packed

2 tablespoons water
2 8-ounce cans crescent
 dinner rolls

Melt butter in small saucepan. Use 2 tablespoons to coat bottom and sides of 12-cup Bundt pan. Sprinkle pan with 3 tablespoons of chopped pecans. Add remaining nuts, brown sugar, and water to remaining butter. Heat to a boil, stirring occasionally. Remove dinner rolls from can but do not unroll. Cut each can of rolls into 16 slices. Arrange 16 slices, cut side up, in bottom of pan, overlapping slices. Separate each slice slightly to allow sauce to penetrate. Spoon half the caramel nut sauce over slices. Repeat next layer with second can of rolls and top with remaining caramel sauce. Bake at 350° for 25-30 minutes or until golden brown. Cool 3 minutes. Turn onto serving platter and slice. Freezes well. Serves 8-10.

Cream Cheese Danish

¾ cup sugar
16 ounces cream cheese,
 softened
1 egg, separated
1 teaspoon vanilla extract

2 tablespoons lemon juice
2 8-ounce cans crescent
 dinner rolls
1 teaspoon water
½ cup slivered almonds

Preheat oven to 350°. Cream sugar and cream cheese until smooth. Add egg yolk, vanilla and lemon juice. Mix until creamy. In 9x13-inch baking pan, unroll 1 package of dinner rolls to cover the pan; seal perforations. Spread cream cheese mixture over dough. Unroll other package of rolls; seal perforations. Place over cream cheese. Mix egg white with water and brush over top of pastry. Sprinkle top with almonds and bake for 30 minutes. Cool 20 minutes and cut into 1x2-inch bars. Yield: 48 bars.

Fresh Fruit with Ginger Crème

7 ounces marshmallow creme
½ cup mayonnaise
½ cup sour cream

¼ teaspoon ground ginger
2 teaspoons grated orange rind
12 cups assorted fresh fruits

Combine all ingredients except fruit and mix until smooth and blended. Prepare fruit in bite-sized pieces. Spoon into serving bowl and serve as a dip with assorted fresh fruit. Yield: 2 cups dip.

Vegetable-Ham Tartlets

1 cup commercial dry biscuit
  mix
1⅔ cups milk
1½ cups grated Monterey Jack
  cheese
1½ cups grated cheddar cheese
5 eggs, beaten
½ teaspoon salt
¼ teaspoon sage
¼ teaspoon thyme
½ teaspoon basil
1 clove garlic, minced
½ cup chopped onion
1 cup sliced fresh mushrooms
10 ounces frozen chopped
  spinach, thawed and well
  drained
1 cup shredded carrots
1 cup finely diced ham

Mix all ingredients together and fill greased miniature muffin tins ⅔ full with mixture. Bake at 375° for 25-30 minutes or until edges begin to pull away from tin. Yield: 48-54 miniature tarts.

Moravian Coffee

¾ pound drip-grind coffee
2 cups sugar
1 pint half-and-half

Put 30 cups of water in large electric percolator. Place coffee in basket of percolator. Perk coffee; remove grounds. Let steep for 1 hour. About 10 minutes before serving, remove small portion of coffee to deep saucepan and add sugar. When sugar is dissolved pour into remaining coffee in percolator, stirring as you pour. Remove small portion of sweetened coffee from percolator to deep saucepan and gradually add half-and-half, stirring constantly. Slowly pour cream mixture into percolator, stirring constantly. Yield: 30 cups.

Chilled Mint Tea

2 cups water
3 family size tea bags
10 fresh mint leaves
1 cup sugar
6 ounces frozen lemonade
6 ounces frozen orange juice

Bring water to a boil. Add tea bags and fresh mint leaves; steep for 10 minutes. Remove tea bags. Add sugar and stir until dissolved. Prepare frozen lemonade and orange juice concentrates according to package directions; stir into sweetened mint tea. Refrigerate overnight. Yield: ½ gallon.

As an additional welcome for the new neighbor, fill an attractive address book with the names, addresses and telephone numbers of her new neighbors, as well as doctors and babysitters. To help her keep in touch with old friends, present her with a gift of stationery personalized with her new address.

NOTES

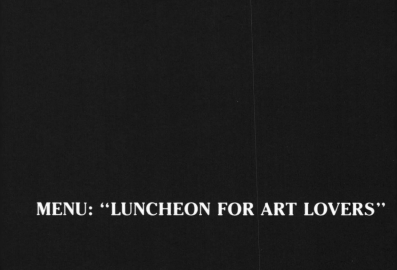

MENU: "LUNCHEON FOR ART LOVERS"

The Ladies' Lunch at Kilgore-Lewis House

Serves 24

Mint Fizz
Cheese Boxes
Pasta Salad Vinaigrette
Fresh Fruit Basket
Pinckney's Bran Muffins
Luscious Lime Mousse
Peaches 'N Cream Cheesecake

Mint Fizz

5 cups water	1 cup fresh mint, chopped
4 cups sugar	6 quarts ginger ale, chilled
4 large oranges	Mint sprigs for garnish
12 medium lemons	

Combine water and sugar and bring to a boil. Boil 10 minutes. Squeeze oranges and lemons. Place juice, rinds and chopped mint in a large container. Pour hot syrup over and stir together. Cover tightly and let stand for 2 hours. Remove rinds; squeeze out juice and strain syrup. Cool and refrigerate until well chilled. May store concentrate up to 3 weeks in refrigerator. When ready to serve, mix concentrate with chilled ginger ale and serve over crushed ice. Garnish with mint sprigs. Yield: 30 cups.

Cheese Boxes

1 cup butter	1 tablespoon milk
½ pound sharp cheddar cheese, grated	½ teaspoon salt
	Tabasco to taste
1 unbeaten egg white	1 loaf white bread, unsliced

Cream cheese and butter until smooth. Add unbeaten egg white, milk, salt and Tabasco. Chill until mixture is spreadable. Remove crust from bread; cut into 1-inch slices. Cut each slice into 4 squares. Place squares on cookie sheet. Spread tops and sides of each square with cheese mixture. Can be frozen at this point. Allow to reach room temperature before baking. Bake at 375° for 15 minutes or until golden brown. Yield: 48 cheese boxes.

Pasta Salad Vinaigrette

2 tablespoons minced garlic
¾ cup Dijon-style mustard
1¼ cups red wine vinegar
4 teaspoons salt
2 teaspoons freshly ground pepper
2 cups walnut oil
1 pound spinach pasta, varied shapes
1 pound egg pasta, varied shapes
1 bunch broccoli

1 pound mushrooms, sliced
3 yellow squash, sliced
3 zucchini squash, sliced
1 small bag radishes, sliced
½ pound green beans, steamed
1 cup grated Parmesan cheese
1 pound bacon, cooked and crumbled
2 cups walnuts, coarsely chopped
Lettuce leaves, optional

Prepare dressing by mixing garlic, mustard, vinegar, salt and pepper in blender. Gradually add walnut oil and process until oil is well-blended. Refrigerate. Cook pasta in boiling salted water until tender. Drain and cool. Wash broccoli and separate into florets. In a large bowl combine cooled pasta with all the vegetables. Pour half of the dressing over the salad and toss until well-mixed. Refrigerate 6-8 hours or overnight. Before serving add Parmesan cheese, bacon, walnuts and additional salad dressing. Salt to taste if more seasoning is needed. Serve salad on lettuce leaf if desired. Serves 24.

Fresh Fruit Basket

1 medium watermelon
4½ cups cantalope balls
4½ cups honeydew melon balls
4 cups fresh strawberries

3 cups cubed fresh pineapple
1 cup fresh blueberries
¾ pound seedless green grapes

Cut watermelon in half; remove seeds. Carefully scoop out fruit balls from watermelon halves, reserving a 1-inch thick shell. Combine watermelon balls with the next 6 ingredients. Toss gently. Fill each melon half with mixed fruit. Yield: 24 servings.

Pinckney's Bran Muffins

6 cups all-bran cereal
2 cups boiling water
1 cup oil
4 eggs, beaten
3 cups sugar
1 quart buttermilk
5 cups plain flour

5 teaspoons baking soda
2 teaspoons salt
24 ounces apple butter
2 cups chopped walnuts, optional
2 cups raisins, optional

Pour the boiling water over 2 cups of bran. Add oil. Mix and let stand while assembling the other ingredients. Mix together beaten eggs, sugar, buttermilk and the rest of the bran in that order. Sift flour with soda and salt. Combine all ingredients, stirring in apple butter, walnuts and raisins last. Bake in greased muffin tins at 400° for 15-20 minutes. Mixture keeps 6 weeks in refrigerator. Muffins freeze well. Yield: 6 dozen.

Luscious Lime Mousse

3 packages unflavored gelatin
1 cup water
4 limes
6 eggs, separated

2 cups sugar
2 teaspoons vanilla extract
3 cups whipping cream
Kiwi, peeled and sliced

Butter crystal sherberts and dust with sugar granules for individual servings. In a saucepan sprinkle gelatin over water. Grate rind of limes. Squeeze limes to yield ¾ cup juice. In top of double boiler, combine egg yolks, sugar, and vanilla. Stir until sugar is melted. Melt gelatin over low heat and add to egg mixture along with lime juice and grated rind. Refrigerate until mixture begins to thicken. Partially whip the whipping cream and refrigerate. Beat egg whites until stiff. Fold partially-whipped cream and egg whites into lime mixture. Ladle into individual crystal sherberts. Refrigerate for at least 2 hours. Garnish with sliced fresh kiwi. Can be prepared in an 8-cup souffle dish with a collar. Need to make recipe twice to serve 24. Serves 12-16.

Peaches 'N Cream Cheesecake

¾ cup plain flour
1 teaspoon baking powder
½ teaspoon salt
1 3-ounce package regular
    vanilla pudding
3 tablespoons butter, softened
1 egg

½ cup milk
1 16-ounce can sliced peaches
8 ounces cream cheese
½ cup sugar
3 tablespoons peach juice
1 tablespoon sugar
½ teaspoon cinnamon

Combine first 7 ingredients in mixing bowl. Mix well. Pour mixture into greased 8-inch round cake pan. Drain peaches, reserving 3 tablespoons of juice. Place well-drained peaches over batter. Combine cream cheese, ½ cup sugar and peach juice; beat for 2 minutes. Spoon mixture to within 1 inch of edge of batter. Combine remaining sugar and cinnamon; sprinkle over cheese filling. Bake at 350° for 30-35 minutes. Filling will appear soft after cooking. Delicious served warm or cold. Sweetened fresh peaches may be substituted. Serves 6.

One of Greenville's landmarks is the Kilgore-Lewis House. Built in 1838, it features hand-blown glass windows, wooden peg construction and copper roofing. This period house was moved to its present site on Academy Street in 1976 and was refurbished. It is adjacent to a spring that was the first water source for Greenville. The Kilgore-Lewis House serves as headquarters for the Greenville Council of Garden Clubs and is maintained by that organization.

Remember the Good Times Lunch

Serves 8

Citrus Sparkler
Swiss Nibbles
Pasta with Panache
Spiced Nut Loaf
Chocolate Mousse Cake

Citrus Sparkler

12 ounces orange juice
    concentrate
 6 ounces lemonade concentrate

6 cups cold water
1 fifth champagne

In large container combine orange juice, lemonade and water. Chill mixture for 12 hours. Before serving combine juices and champagne. Serve from crystal pitcher. Serves 24.

Swiss Nibbles

½ cup hot water
¼ cup butter
⅛ teaspoon salt
⅛ teaspoon sugar
½ cup plain flour

¾ teaspoon dry mustard
    Dash cayenne pepper
2 eggs
½ cup shredded Swiss cheese

In small saucepan, combine water, butter, salt and sugar. Cook until butter melts and mixture boils. Vigorously stir in flour, dry mustard and cayenne. Stir over medium heat until mixture leaves sides of pan. Remove from heat and stir in eggs, one at a time, until blended. Stir in cheese. Drop from teaspoon onto greased baking sheet. Can be prepared to this point and baked when needed. Bake at 450° for 10 minutes. Reduce heat to 375° and bake 15 minutes, until puffed and golden. Turn oven off and let puffs remain inside 3 more minutes. Serve hot. Yield: 20 appetizers.

Pasta with Panache

 1 pound raw shrimp
 1 pound fresh asparagus
30 large basil leaves, fresh
 4 cloves garlic, finely chopped
 2 cups cream
 1 cup butter
16 ounces fresh fettucine

2 cups grated Parmesan cheese
   Salt and pepper to taste
   Nutmeg to taste
   Basil
   Lemon wedges
   Red lettuce leaves

continued

Peel, devein and butterfly shrimp. Cook asparagus and cut into 1-inch pieces. In large saucepan, combine basil, garlic, cream and butter. Bring to a boil and simmer until thickened. Meanwhile, bring 4 quarts water to a boil. Add noodles and cook 8-10 minutes or until al dente. Add shrimp and asparagus to cream sauce. Cook shrimp 6-8 minutes or until pink. Drain noodles and toss into cream mixture. Add cheese, salt, pepper and nutmeg. Serve garnished with basil leaves and lemon wedges on a bed of red lettuce leaves. Serves 8.

Spiced Nut Loaf

3½ cups sifted plain flour	4 eggs, beaten
2 teaspoons soda	⅔ cups water
1½ teaspoons salt	1 cup salad oil
2 teaspoons cinnamon	1 pound can pumpkin
2 teaspoons nutmeg	1 cup chopped pecans
3 cups sugar	

In a large mixing bowl, combine all dry ingredients. Add eggs, water, oil and pumpkin. Stir until well mixed. Add nuts and pour mixture into 3 greased and floured loaf pans. Bake 1 hour at 350°. Cool and turn out on rack. To serve, cut loaf into 1-inch slices. Cut each slice diagonally and place 2 triangles on rim of each plate. Bread will keep in refrigerator several weeks or may be frozen. Yield: 3 loaves.

Chocolate Mousse Cake

7 ounces semi-sweet chocolate chips	1 teaspoon vanilla extract
½ cup unsalted butter	⅛ teaspoon cream of tartar
7 eggs, separated	1 cup whipping cream
1 cup sugar, divided	⅓ cup powdered sugar
	1 teaspoon vanilla extract

Preheat oven to 325°. Melt chocolate and butter in saucepan or microwave. Beat egg yolks. Add ¾ cup of sugar and beat until fluffy, about 5 minutes. Gradually beat in chocolate/butter mixture and vanilla. Beat egg whites with cream of tartar until soft peaks form adding ¼ cup sugar, 1 tablespoon at a time. Fold egg whites carefully into chocolate mixture. Pour ¾ of batter into 8-inch spring form pan. Cover and refrigerate remaining batter. Bake cake for 35 minutes. Remove cake and cool. Cake will fall. Pour remaining batter onto cooled cake. Refrigerate until firm, about 8 hours or overnight. Prepare frosting by beating cream with powdered sugar and vanilla until stiff. Spread frosting on cake. Garnish with grated chocolate. Serves 8-10.

The Spiced Nut Loaf is a wonderful gift from the kitchen that refrigerates well or can be frozen. Try it for a morning club meeting served with coffee.

For a Special Saturday

Serves 12

Cream of Artichoke Soup
Marinated Beef Salad
Mom's Blueberry Muffins
Lemon Sandwiches
Grasshopper Soufflé

Cream of Artichoke Soup

4 14-ounce cans artichoke
hearts
2 10½-ounce cans mushroom
soup
2 cups half-and-half

2 cups chicken broth
2 teaspoons salt
1 teaspoon pepper
½ cup dry white wine

Drain artichoke hearts and chop in food processor. Combine mushroom soup, half-and-half, and chicken broth; stir over low heat until smooth. Add artichoke hearts, salt, pepper, and white wine. Heat and serve. May be refrigerated for several days. Serves 12.

Marinated Beef Salad

3½ pounds cooked roast beef
1 large white onion, thinly sliced
and separated into rings
2 cups water
¼ teaspoon salt
1 teaspoon lemon juice
12 ounces fresh mushrooms
1 cup red wine vinegar
5 teaspoons Dijon-style mustard
2 teaspoons salt

½ teaspoon dried marjoram,
crushed
½ teaspoon dried parsley,
crushed
½ teaspoon freshly ground
pepper
2 cups salad oil
Lettuce leaves
¼ cup chopped fresh parsley

Chill beef and cut into thin strips. Cut onion into thin slices and separate into rings. In saucepan, combine water, salt and lemon juice. Bring to boil. Drop in onion rings. Remove immediately and drain on paper towels. Cut mushrooms into thick slices. Arrange meat, onion rings and mushrooms in 13x9x2-inch dish. Stir together vinegar, mustard, remaining salt, herbs and pepper. Gradually blend in oil. Pour over beef and vegetables; cover with plastic wrap. Chill several hours or overnight, basting occasionally. Before serving, remove meat, onion rings and mushrooms from marinade and arrange on lettuce-lined serving platter. Sprinkle fresh parsley on top before serving. Serves 12.

Mom's Blueberry Muffins

½ cup butter
1 cup sugar
2 eggs
½ teaspoon vanilla extract
2 cups plain flour

2 teaspoons baking powder
½ teaspoon salt
½ cup milk
2½ cups blueberries
¼ cup sugar

Cream butter and 1 cup sugar until fluffy. Add eggs 1 at a time. Stir in vanilla. Add dry ingredients alternately with milk and mix well. Add blueberries. Grease pan and fill muffin cups full. Sprinkle tops with remaining ¼ cup of sugar. Bake at 350° for 35 minutes or until lightly browned. Cool 30 minutes before removing from pan. Yield: 16 muffins.

Lemon Sandwiches

3 egg yolks
½ cup sugar
  Juice and rind of 2 lemons
8 ounces cream cheese,
  softened

1 cup pecans, crushed
20 thin slices whole wheat bread
  Mayonnaise

Cook egg yolks, sugar, lemon juice and rind over medium heat until thick, stirring constantly. Add cream cheese and pecans. Stir until smooth. Refrigerate. Remove from refrigerator 30 minutes before making sandwiches. Trim crust from bread. Whole wheat bread is preferred. Spread mayonnaise on bread slices. Spread lemon filling on slices and make sandwiches. Cut sandwiches diagonally. Yield: 20 sandwich triangles.

Grasshopper Soufflé

2 envelopes unflavored gelatin
1 cup cold water
1 cup sugar, divided
¼ teaspoon salt
6 eggs, separated

½ cup creme de menthe
½ cup white cream de cacao
2 cups heavy cream, whipped
  Semi-sweet chocolate

Sprinkle gelatin over water in 2½-quart pan. Add ½ cup sugar, salt and egg yolks. Place over low heat, stirring until gelatin dissolves and mixture thickens slightly, about 5 minutes. Remove from heat; stir in creme de menthe and creme de cacao. Chill, stirring occasionally until mixture mounds slightly when dropped from spoon. Beat egg whites in large bowl until stiff but not dry. Gradually add remaining sugar and beat until very stiff. Fold in gelatin mixture. Fold in whipped cream. Add 2-inch collar to 2½-quart souffle dish. Pour in mixture and chill. Remove collar and garnish with chocolate curls before serving. Serves 12.

Lunching in Hampton-Pinckney

Serves 16

Broccoli-Cream Cheese Soup
Crab Cheese Puffs
Seasonal Fruit Kabobs
Mocha Frosted Orange Chiffon

Broccoli-Cream Cheese Soup

1 cup chopped green onion
4 tablespoons butter
.32 ounces cream cheese
4 cups half-and-half
4 cups chicken broth
6 10-ounce packages frozen
  chopped broccoli

2 teaspoons lemon juice
2 teaspoons salt
1 teaspoon pepper
  Slivered almonds
  Fresh parsley

Saute green onions in butter in large saucepan or Dutch oven. Cube cream cheese. Add cubed cheese and cream to onions and stir over low heat until cheese is melted. Stir in chicken broth; set aside. Cook broccoli according to package directions and drain. Blend ½ of broccoli mixture in food processor or blender until smooth. Add processed broccoli and remaining chopped broccoli to soup mixture. Stir in lemon juice and seasonings. Heat thoroughly. Toast almonds. Before serving, top each bowl of soup with toasted almonds and a sprig of parsley. Serves 16.

Crab Cheese Puffs

1 cup butter, softened
2 5-ounce jars processed sharp
  cheese spread
½ teaspoon garlic salt

3 teaspoons mayonnaise
2 cups fresh crab meat
12 English muffins, split

Cream butter and cheese together. Mix in garlic salt and mayonnaise. Stir in crab meat. Spread mixture on muffin halves. Prepared muffin halves may be placed on cookie sheet and frozen; store muffins in plastic bags until ready to use. When ready to serve, place muffin halves on cookie sheet and broil until lightly browned. Yield: 24 muffin halves.

Seasonal Fruit Kabobs

2 pints strawberries
1 7-ounce can pineapple chunks

8 kiwi, peeled and sliced
2 cantalopes, cubed

Spear pineapple, strawberry, kiwi and cantaloupe on long toothpick to create a fruit kabob. May select other firm fruits or melons in season. Serves 16.

Mocha Frosted Orange Chiffon

2 cups plain flour
1½ cups sugar
3 teaspoons baking powder
1 teaspoon salt
½ cup oil
7 egg yolks
¾ cup cold water
2 tablespoons grated orange rind
7 egg whites, room temperature

½ teaspoon cream of tartar
1 3½-ounce package instant chocolate pudding mix
1 2.8-ounce box of whipped topping mix
1½ tablespoon instant coffee granules
1¾ cups milk
1 cup finely chopped pecans

Sift together flour, sugar, baking powder and salt in a mixing bowl. Make a well in the center; add oil, yolks, water and grated rind. Beat at high speed of electric mixer 5 minutes or until satin smooth. Combine egg whites and cream of tartar in a large mixing bowl; beat until stiff peaks form. Pour egg yolk mixture in a thin steady stream over entire surface of egg whites; gently fold yolk mixture into whites. Pour batter into an ungreased 10-inch tube pan, spreading batter evenly with a spatula. Bake at 325° for 1 hour and 15 minutes or until cake springs back when touched. Remove from oven; invert pan, and cool completely before removing from pan. To prepare frosting combine pudding mix, topping mix, coffee and milk in a mixing bowl and beat at high speed until stiff. Cut cake into 3 layers. Frost each layer with mocha mixture and sprinkle with chopped nuts. Frost top and sides of cake with remaining frosting and sprinkle top of cake liberally with remaining nuts. Keep refrigerated. Serves 16.

The Hampton-Pinckney Historic District, located in the heart of downtown Greenville, reflects the beauty of homes built in the late nineteenth and early twentieth centuries. Many of the forty-seven structures in the District have been restored to their original state. The area, one of Greenville's older existing residential neighborhoods, was part of the home garden of Vardry McBee, an early developer of Greenville. In December of 1977, the Hampton-Pinckney Historic District was placed on The National Register of Historic Places.

Buffet Luncheon for Baby's Christening

Serves 8

Pineapple Glazed Ham
Brown Sugared Grapes
Light Mustard Sauce for Ham
Cauliflower-Pea Casserole
Waldorf Salad
Something Extra Soufflé
Sweet Potato Biscuits
Lemon Daffodil Dessert

Pineapple Glazed Ham

4 pound cured ham
  Whole cloves
1 8-ounce can crushed
  pineapple, with juice
½ cup brown sugar, firmly
  packed

2 tablespoons honey
1 tablespoon dry mustard
2 tablespoons corn starch

Place ham, fat side up, on a large piece of aluminum foil in a shallow roasting pan. Wrap foil loosely around ham. Bake at 325°, about 25 minutes per pound. Remove ham from oven 30 minutes before cooking time is up. Remove any skin and score ham in a diamond pattern, making cuts ¼ inch deep in ham fat. Place 1 whole clove in center of each diamond. To prepare pineapple glaze combine remaining ingredients in saucepan and cook over medium heat; stir constantly until mixture boils. Continue to stir and boil for 1 minute. Spoon glaze over ham and return to oven. Bake, uncovered, at 375° for 30 minutes or until glaze is bubbly, basting frequently. Serve ham on platter garnished with frosted grapes. Serves 8-10.

Brown Sugared Grapes

1½ pounds seedless green grapes
½ cup sour cream

¼ cup brown sugar

Wash and dry grapes. Mix them with sour cream. Sprinkle with brown sugar before serving.

Light Mustard Sauce for Ham

¼ cup sugar
2 tablespoons dry mustard
½ teaspoon salt

2 egg yolks, beaten
1 13-ounce can evaporated milk
½ cup vinegar

Combine first 4 ingredients in top of a double boiler. Gradually add evaporated milk and stir until smooth. Cook mixture until smooth and thickened, stirring constantly. Stir in vinegar and cook until creamy. Serve hot over ham slices. Yield: 2 cups.

Cauliflower-Pea Casserole

1 large head cauliflower
2 10-ounce packages frozen
  English peas
3 tablespoons butter
2 tablespoons flour

1½ cups sour cream
1 teaspoon onion salt
½ teaspoon curry powder
½ cup sliced almonds

Steam cauliflower and drain. Cook peas and drain. Melt 1½ tablespoons butter; add flour and cook for 1 minute. Add sour cream and stir until well heated. Add onion salt. Gently stir in the cauliflower and peas. Place mixture in a buttered 9-inch casserole dish. To make topping melt 1½ tablespoons butter and stir in curry powder and almonds. Pour over casserole and bake at 350° for 30 minutes or until bubbly. Serves 8.

Waldorf Salad

4 large Red Delicious apples,
  coarsely chopped
4 large Yellow Delicious apples,
  coarsely chopped
1 cup seedless grapes, red or
  green

½ cup raisins
1 cup coarsely chopped
  walnuts
1 cup mayonnaise
⅓ cup half-and-half
3 tablespoons sugar

Mix mayonnaise, half-and-half and sugar; toss with fruit and nuts. Serves 8-10.

Something Extra Soufflé

½ cup hot water
6 slices bread, crust removed
1 13-ounce can evaporated milk
3 eggs, beaten
1 4-ounce jar chopped pimentos

1 pound sharp cheddar cheese,
  grated
  Salt and red pepper to taste
5 tablespoons butter

Combine bread with hot water to make paste. Add milk, eggs, pimentos, cheese, salt and pepper. Melt butter in a 2-quart baking dish; pour in all ingredients and mix well. Bake about 1½ hours at 250° until lightly browned. Serves 8.

Sweet Potato Biscuits

3 cups flour
¾ cup sugar
1 tablespoon salt
3 teaspoons baking powder
1½ teaspoons allspice

1 teaspoon cinnamon
¾ cup shortening
2 cups mashed sweet potatoes
⅓ cup milk
Flour

Mix dry ingredients together. Cut in shortening until mixture resembles coarse meal. Stir in sweet potatoes. Add milk and stir until dry ingredients are moistened. Turn dough out onto floured surface; roll to ½-inch thickness. Cut dough with 2-inch biscuit cutter. Place on greased cookie pan and bake at 450° for 12-15 minutes. Yield: 18-20 biscuits.

Lemon Daffodil Dessert

Juice of 4 lemons
½ cup sugar
1 14-ounce can condensed milk

2 cups whipping cream
1 small commercial angel food cake

Combine juice, sugar and milk. Add whipped cream. Tear cake into small pieces and line the bottom of a 9x13x2-inch baking dish. Pour mixture over the cake and mix together a little. Chill for 24 hours before serving. Serves 8-10.

This menu leaves few last minute details. The day before completely prepare ham, mustard sauce, biscuits, and dessert. Assemble soufflé and casserole to bake the next day. The salad is best when prepared several hours prior to serving.

Fall Bridge Luncheon

Serves 8

Mediterranean Tart
Broccoli Mold with Lemon Sauce
Autumn Salad
Pumpkin Cheesecake

Mediterranean Tart

3 tablespoons butter
1 onion, chopped fine
1 cup sliced mushrooms
¼ teaspoon thyme
2 tablespoons flour
1 cup chicken broth
2 tomatoes, peeled, seeded, chopped
4 pound chicken, cooked and cubed

½ pound ham, chopped
½ cup pitted black olives, chopped
   Salt and pepper to taste
¾ cup unsalted butter, melted
16 (16x12-inch) sheets phyllo dough
½ cup grated Parmesan cheese

Melt butter. Add onions and saute until clear. Add mushrooms and thyme and cook 5 minutes. Blend flour and cook 2-3 minutes stirring frequently. Add chicken broth and tomatoes and cook until thickened, stirring constantly. Reduce heat; add chicken, ham and olives and simmer for 5 minutes. Add salt and pepper. Let cool. Preheat oven to 300°. Brush bottom and sides of 16x12-inch casserole dish with melted butter. Line dish with 1 sheet phyllo, pressing firmly into corners and sides of dish. Brush with melted butter being sure to reach into corners and sides. Repeat until 8 sheets of phyllo are in dish. Spoon filling over phyllo, spreading into corners. Sprinkle with all the cheese. Top with a sheet of phyllo and brush with butter. Repeat with remaining phyllo. Trim excess phyllo from edges of dish using scissors. Brush top with remaining butter. Bake, brush with butter several times until pastry is crisp and golden, about 1 hour. Cut into squares and serve immediately. Serves 8.

Broccoli Mold with Lemon Sauce

Bread crumbs
½ cup chopped onion
2 tablespoons butter
2 10½-ounce packages chopped
　frozen broccoli
1 cup shredded Swiss cheese
⅔ cup bread crumbs
　Salt and pepper to taste
½ teaspoon nutmeg
1 cup milk

4 tablespoons butter
5 eggs, beaten
2 cups chicken stock
4 tablespoons butter
4 tablespoons flour
2 tablespoons lemon juice
　Salt and pepper to taste
2 egg yolks
　Steamed carrots, optional

Preheat oven to 325°. Line a 6-cup souffle or ring mold with waxpaper, then oil and cover with bread crumbs. Saute onions in 2 tablespoons butter, then add frozen chopped broccoli and cook until half done. Place this mixture in a bowl with Swiss cheese, bread crumbs, salt, pepper and nutmeg, then mix. Bring milk to a boil with 4 tablespoons butter. Slowly add this to the eggs. Add this custard to broccoli mixture and then fill the mold. Place mold in a pan filled with boiling water and bake 1 hour. Heat chicken stock for lemon sauce. In separate saucepan, make a roux with butter and flour. Cook at least 2 minutes, but do not brown. Remove from heat and pour in hot chicken stock all at once. Add lemon juice, salt and pepper. Enrich the sauce by beating in 2 egg yolks. Let broccoli mold set 5 minutes then unmold and serve with lemon sauce. Center of mold may be filled with steamed carrots. Serves 8.

Autumn Salad

3 Granny Smith apples, chilled
3 Red Delicious apples, chilled
⅔ cup sherry vinegar
1½ cups chopped celery
½ cup walnut halves

¼ cup blond raisins
½ cup green grapes, sliced
3 spring onions, chopped
4 tablespoons walnut oil

Wash apples and dry well. Core and chop, but do not peel them. Toss apples in a bowl with the sherry vinegar. Add celery, walnut halves, raisins, green grapes and onions; drizzle with the walnut oil. Toss again. Taste and correct the seasoning, adding more vinegar and up to a tablespoon more oil as necessary. Serve immediately. Serves 8.

Pumpkin Cheesecake

1 cup uncooked quick oatmeal
⅓ cup brown sugar
4 tablespoons butter, melted
½ teaspoon cinnamon
⅓ cup chopped pecans
32 ounces cream cheese

4 cups sugar
5 eggs
1 18-ounce can pumpkin pie mix
3 tablespoons pumpkin pie spice
1 cup whipping cream, whipped
2 tablespoons powdered sugar

Preheat oven to 475°. Mix together the first 5 ingredients. Press into a greased 9-inch springform pan and bake 8-10 minutes, or until golden. Lower oven temperature to 325°. Beat cream cheese with mixer until smooth and fluffy. Add the sugar and continue beating. Add eggs, 1 at a time, beating well after each addition. Add pumpkin pie mix and spice; mix well. Pour into crust and bake at 325° for 1 hour 45 minutes. Refrigerate at least 12 hours. Before serving top with whipped cream, sweetened with powdered sugar. Serves 12-15.

This is an excellent menu for entertaining in the fall when apples and pumpkins are plentiful. The Autumn Salad is pretty served in red leaf lettuce cups and garnished with unpeeled apple slices. For additional seasonal flair, garnish the Pumpkin Cheesecake with candy corn or pumpkins.

Rainy Day "Pick Me Up" Lunch

Serves 8

Sausage and Lentil Soup
Caesar Salad
Golden Sesame Twigs
Apple Clafouti

Sausage and Lentil Soup

2 cups lentils, rinsed and culled
½ teaspoon thyme
½ teaspoon oregano
½ teaspoon basil
1 bay leaf
1 pound bulk smoked sausage

1 pound Italian sausage
1 28-ounce can plum tomatoes
1 cup chopped onion
7 cups water
1 10¾-ounce can beef broth

In a kettle, cover lentils with water and add seasonings. Bring water to a boil, skimming the froth as it rises. Simmer the mixture, covered for about 40 minutes. In a large skillet, brown sausage meat, crumbled, over moderately high heat. Transfer it with a slotted spoon to the kettle and pour off the fat in the skillet. In skillet over moderate heat, brown the Italian sausage, pricked lightly but not sliced. Transfer sausage with the slotted spoon to cutting board and cut into ½-inch sections. Add sausage to kettle with tomatoes, drained and chopped and onion. Add 7 cups water and beef broth. Bring to boil and simmer 10 minutes. Serves 8.

Caesar Salad

½ cup fresh Parmesan cheese, grated
½ cup oil
1 egg
2 tablespoons fresh lemon juice
1 teaspoon Worcestershire sauce

1 clove garlic, crushed
1 teaspoon pepper
1 head Romaine lettuce
1 head Bibb lettuce
Seasoned croutons

Combine cheese, oil, egg, lemon juice, Worcestershire, garlic and pepper in blender and process for 6 seconds. Toss dressing with the lettuce and croutons and serve immediately. Serves 8.

Golden Sesame Twigs

2 cups plain flour
2 teaspoons baking powder
½ teaspoon salt
5 tablespoons shortening

⅔ cup milk
3 tablespoons butter, melted
¼ cup sesame seed

Combine flour, baking powder and salt. Cut in shortening until mixture resembles coarse meal. Add milk, stirring until moistened. Turn dough onto a lightly floured surface. Knead 3-4 times. Roll dough into a rectangle ¼-inch thick. Cut into 1x3-inch strips. Place strips on greased baking sheet. Brush strips with butter and sprinkle with sesame seed. Bake at 350° for 10-12 minutes or until golden. Yield: 30 sticks.

Apple Clafouti

2 large apples, peeled and cored
2 tablespoons butter
2 tablespoons almond extract
1 tablespoon lemon juice
½ cup flour
½ teaspoon baking powder

¼ teaspoon salt
¼ cup honey
¼ cup heavy cream
2 eggs
Confectioners' sugar

Cut apples into ¼-inch wedges. Melt butter in skillet and simmer apples with almond extract and lemon juice 5 minutes or until apples are almost tender. Remove from heat; cool. In medium bowl mix flour, baking powder and salt. Stir in honey, cream and eggs until smooth and blended. Pour ⅓ batter in greased shallow baking dish or 9-inch pie plate; spread evenly. Bake in preheated 400° oven until set, 3 to 4 minutes. Arrange apple mixture on top; pour on remaining batter; spread evenly. Bake 20 to 25 minutes longer or until puffed and golden. Sprinkle with confectioners' sugar. Cut in wedges. Serve immediately with warm honey. Serves 8.

Luncheon for Art Lovers

Serves 8

Golden Harvest Cauliflower Soup
Mandarin Toss Salad
Spicy Bacon Spears
Bacon Stiks
Sour Cream Apple Pie

Golden Harvest Cauliflower Soup

1 large head cauliflower	1 pound cooked ham
4 cups water	1 cup instant potato flakes
16 ounces cream cheese, cubed	
8 ounces processed cheese spread	

Wash cauliflower and break into small flowerets. Steam until tender and set aside. Combine water, cream cheese, cheese spread and potato flakes in top of double boiler. Stir over boiling water until mixture is smooth. Cut ham into Julienne strips. Stir ham and cauliflower into soup and cook until thoroughly heated. Serves 8.

Mandarin Toss Salad

½ cup oil	1 head Bibb lettuce
4 tablespoons sugar	4 green onions with tops, sliced
2 tablespoons vinegar	2 11-ounce cans mandarin oranges
2 tablespoons chopped parsley	1 cup chopped pecans, toasted
1 teaspoon salt	1 avocado, peeled and sliced
Dash of pepper	Fresh pepper
Dash of red pepper sauce	
1 bunch Romaine lettuce	

To prepare dressing combine first 7 ingredients in covered jar and shake well; refrigerate. To prepare salad, tear lettuce into bite-size pieces and place in salad bowl. Add green onion and drained orange segments. Before serving add pecans and avocado. Grind fresh pepper over salad liberally. Pour dressing over salad and toss. Best if served immediately for maximum crispness. Serves 8.

Spicy Bacon Spears

1½ cups grated sharp cheese
½ cup mayonnaise
2 tablespoons chopped bell peppers
1 tablespoon grated onion
1 teaspoon Worcestershire sauce
1 teaspoon dry mustard
¼ teaspoon salt
4 hot dog buns
8 bacon slices

Combine cheese, mayonnaise, peppers, onion, Worcestershire sauce and salt. Separate hot dog buns and split each lengthwise. Split bacon lengthwise and cook on one side only. Spread cheese mixture on bread strips. Top with bacon, uncooked side up, and broil until bacon cooks and cheese melts. Yield: 16 spears.

Bacon Stiks

18 thin commercial bread sticks
1 cup grated Parmesan cheese
9 slices bacon, halved lengthwise

Dredge 1 side of bacon slices in cheese. Wrap cheese side of bacon diagonally around bread stick. Place sticks on microwave dish lined with paper towel. Microwave on high for 4½ to 6 minutes. Remove sticks and roll in additional cheese. Yield: 18 sticks.

Sour Cream Apple Pie

1 9-inch pie shell
¾ cup sugar
¾ cup firmly packed brown sugar
1 tablespoon plain flour
½ teaspoon ground cinnamon
¼ teaspoon ground nutmeg
⅛ teaspoon salt
1 teaspoon fresh lemon juice
½ cup sour cream
4 cups apples, peeled and sliced
½ cup plain flour
4 tablespoons butter, softened

Preheat oven to 350°. In a large bowl, combine sugar, ¼ cup brown sugar, 1 tablespoon of flour, spices, salt and lemon juice. Add sour cream and apples. Spoon mixture into unbaked pie crust and set aside. Mix together ½ cup plain flour and ½ cup brown sugar. Cut in butter with fork until mixture is crumbly. Sprinkle topping over pie and bake for 40 minutes. Chill 3 to 4 hours before serving. Serves 8.

Greenville's rich appreciation for the arts offers a bounty of exhibits to satisfy the appetite of the heartiest art lover. The Greenville County Museum of Art is nationally renowned for the largest collection of Andrew Wyeth paintings outside the artist's own holdings.

Bob Jones University Gallery of Sacred Art features one of the world's best known collections of religious art dating from the 13th through the 19th centuries.

Reedy River Run Repast

Serves 8

Chilled Cucumber Soup
Crunchy Cheese Sandwiches
Seasonal Fruit with Whipped Dressing
Memama's Chocolate Pie

Chilled Cucumber Soup

1 small cucumber, unpeeled
3 large cucumbers, peeled and seeded
4 cups chicken broth
1 leek

1 cup spinach leaves, uncooked
Salt and pepper to taste
1 teaspoon dill
1 teaspoon dried parsley
½ cup sour cream or yogurt

Slice small cucumber and set aside for garnish. Slice large cucumbers and add to chicken broth. Cut leek in 3 or 4 slices and add to broth. Allow mixture to come to a boil; reduce heat and simmer for 30 minutes. Remove vegetables from broth and process, or put in blender and puree. Add spinach leaves and chop until fine. Return all vegetables to broth and season with salt, pepper, dill and parsley. Serve cold with dollop of sour cream or yogurt. Garnish each serving with cucumber slice. Serves 8.

Crunchy Cheese Sandwiches

8 ounces cheddar cheese, grated
8 ounces cottage cheese
½ cup garbanzo beans, drained
½ cup chopped celery
½ cup black olives, drained

½ cup chopped pecans
1 tablespoon grated onion, optional
½ cup mayonnaise
⅓ cup sour cream

Chop garbanzo beans and olives. In mixing bowl, combine cheeses, garbanzo beans, celery, olives, pecans and onion. Stir in mayonnaise and sour cream. Chill well. Prepare sandwiches using whole grain bread of your choice. Yield: 8-10 sandwiches.

Seasonal Fruit with Whipped Dressing

1 large lemon	1 egg, well beaten
1 large orange	1 cup heavy cream, whipped
1 cup sugar	Seasonal fresh fruit

Grate rind of lemon and orange. Juice lemon and orange. Put grated rinds and juices in top of double boiler. Add sugar. Cook, stirring occasionally until sugar is dissolved. Whisking briskly, add a little of hot syrup to egg. Whisk mixture and add this to remaining hot syrup. Cook in double boiler until thickened. Fold above ingredients into heavy cream; refrigerate. Mixture will thicken slightly as it cools. Serve over fresh fruit. Yield: 2½ cups.

Memama's Chocolate Pie

24 vanilla wafers	5 ounces evaporated milk
4 tablespoons butter	⅛ teaspoon salt
1 cup sugar	1 tablespoon butter
1½ tablespoons cocoa powder	1 teaspoon vanilla extract
3 tablespoons flour	1 cup whipping cream, whipped
1 egg yolk	2 tablespoons powdered sugar

Preheat oven to 350°. Crumble vanilla wafers. Place 4 tablespoons of butter in 8-inch pie pan and melt in oven. Add crumbled wafers and mix well, patting firmly to make pie crust. Bake 10 minutes or until golden brown. Meanwhile place sugar, cocoa and flour in saucepan over medium heat. Mix until blended. Add egg yolk and milk gradually, stirring constantly. Add salt and 1 tablespoon butter and cook until thick, stirring constantly. Bring to a boil and let it cook for 3-5 minutes. Remove from heat. Add vanilla. Pour into hot pie crust. Cool at least 1 hour. Top with whipped cream, sweetened with powdered sugar. Serves 8.

A springtime favorite in Greenville for runners and spectators alike is the annual Reedy River Run which is sponsored by South Carolina National Bank and directed by the Greenville Track Club. The race is one of twenty on the Grand Prix Circuit and is acclaimed by Racing South magazine as the toughest course on the circuit. The race, which started in 1978, has had as many as 1,400 competitors and attracts national as well as local enthusiasts. An attraction for Olympic class runners is the prize monies awarded to the top male and female finishers according to Athletic's Congress Guidelines.

Greenville Woman's Club Luncheon

Serves 12

Chicken Salad Croissants
Spinach Salad with Strawberries
Cheesy Carrot Fingers
Chocolate Éclair Squares

Chicken Salad Croissants

8 chicken breast halves, cooked
1¼ cups diced celery
4 hard-cooked eggs, chopped
Juice of 1 lemon
Salt to taste
½ teaspoon white pepper
Paprika to taste
1½ cups mayonnaise
¾ cup chopped pecans
12 bakery croissants
Watercress or parsley for garnish

Cut chicken into small cubes. Combine chicken, celery, eggs, lemon juice, seasonings and mayonnaise together; refrigerate overnight. Just before serving stir in chopped pecans and adjust seasonings. Slice croissants partially through from inside curve to outside and warm uncovered in 350° oven for 5-8 minutes. Fill warm croissants with a generous portion of chilled chicken salad and place on plate with a sprig of watercress or parsley for garnish. Serves 12.

Spinach Salad with Strawberries

1½ cups sugar
1½ teaspoons paprika
¾ teaspoon dry mustard
1½ teaspoons Worcestershire sauce
1½ cups oil
1½ teaspoons minced onion
¾ cup vinegar
⅓ cup poppy seeds
⅓ cup sesame seeds, toasted
1 pound fresh spinach
1 pint fresh strawberries, sliced
4 medium bananas, sliced
1 cup chopped walnuts

Prepare dressing by combining sugar, paprika, mustard, Worcestershire, oil, onion, vinegar and seeds in a blender; process until well mixed. Layer torn spinach, fruits and nuts on plate and top with dressing. Serves 12.

Cheesy Carrot Fingers

12 medium carrots, washed and
    scraped
1½ cups grated sharp cheddar
    cheese
4 tablespoons grated onion

1 teaspoon seasoned salt
4 teaspoons Dijon-style mustard
1 cup seasoned buttered bread
    crumbs

Boil carrots in salted water for 5 minutes or until tender. Remove several inches from tapered end of each carrot and mash until smooth. Split remaining carrot piece lengthwise; hollow center with a spoon and discard pulp. Combine mashed carrots with grated cheese, onion, seasoned salt and mustard. Mix well and stuff into hollowed carrots. Top with buttered bread crumbs and brown in 325° oven for 20 minutes. This can be made the day before and refrigerated until ready to cook. Serves 12.

Chocolate Éclair Squares

1 14-ounce box graham crackers
2 4-ounce packages instant
    vanilla pudding
3 cups milk
12 ounces nondairy whipped
    topping
3 ounces semi-sweet chocolate
    chips

2 teaspoons light corn syrup
3 teaspoons butter
1 teaspoon vanilla extract
1½ cup sifted powdered sugar
3 tablespoons milk

Line a 9x13x2-inch glass dish with whole graham crackers. Using milk, prepare pudding according to package directions. Fold nondairy topping into pudding. Spread half of pudding mixture over graham crackers. Repeat cracker and pudding mixture layers. Then top with layer of crackers. To prepare icing, melt chocolate chips, syrup and butter. Stir in vanilla, sugar and milk. Ice pie and refrigerate overnight. Serves 12-16.

The house now called The Woman's Club was the home of the Beattie family for 104 years from 1834 until 1938. Refurbished and relocated on Church Street, the Woman's Club facilities now house social and cultural events for its members and private events such as wedding receptions, luncheons and teas.

Cottage Luncheon

Serves 12

Hot Chicken Salad Pie
Fresh Broccoli Salad à la Fran
Seeded Bread Sticks
Chocolate Almond Crème

Hot Chicken Salad Pie

3 cups cooked chicken, diced
2 cups cooked rice
1 medium onion, chopped
½ cup chopped celery
1 can cream of mushroom soup
1 cup mayonnaise
4 tablespoons lemon juice
2 teaspoons salt
4 hard-cooked eggs, grated
2 9-inch deep dish pie shells
2 cups crushed cornflakes
4 tablespoons butter, melted

Mix all ingredients except pie shells, cornflakes and butter. Refrigerate overnight or several hours. Pre-cook the deep dish pie shells for 10 minutes at 400°. Fill pie shells with chicken mixture and bake 40 minutes at 350°. Melt 4 tablespoons butter and saute cornflakes. Sprinkle this topping over 2 pies and bake 5 more minutes. Each pie serves 6.

Fresh Broccoli Salad à la Fran

1½ bunches fresh broccoli
1 12-ounce jar stuffed green
olives, drained
1 small onion
3 hard-cooked eggs
4 tablespoons mayonnaise
Seasoning salt to taste
Pepper to taste
Lettuce leaves

Wash broccoli and trim ends. In food processor begin to chop the stems which have been cut into small pieces. Do not over process but make the broccoli about the texture of slaw. Chop the flowerets last. In the processor work bowl, finely chop well-drained stuffed green olives, the small onion, and 2-3 hard-cooked eggs. Make all ingredients about the same texture. Add mayonnaise just to bind, or to taste. Add the seasoning salt and black pepper. Chill well and serve on lettuce leaves. Serves 12.

Seeded Bread Sticks

1 stick butter, softened
½ teaspoon salt
½ teaspoon paprika
1 teaspoon celery seed
2 teaspoons sesame seeds

½ teaspoon caraway or poppy
 seeds
Dash cayenne
8 hot dog buns, split

Mix all the above ingredients and spread on hot dog buns. Cut rounded ends off buns. Cut each half lengthwise into 3 sticks. Bake 325° oven until crisp. Yield: 48 bread sticks.

Chocolate Almond Crème

4 cups whipping cream
1 14-ounce can condensed milk
1 16-ounce can chocolate syrup
2 tablespoons vanilla extract

4 teaspoons almond extract
1 2½-ounce package sliced
 almonds

Put all ingredients except nuts in mixer bowl. Chill thoroughly in refrigerator for at least 1½ hours. Remove from refrigerator and beat with electric mixer until peaks are formed. Do not over-beat or mixture gets buttery. Toast almonds. May add nuts after toasting and fold into the mixture or may sprinkle them on top of each portion when served. Put in 5-ounce plastic tumblers or if using paper baking cups, set in muffin tins until frozen. Must be frozen ahead of time. Take immediately from freezer and serve. Serves 24.

One of Greenville's oldest buildings is Falls Cottage which was built in 1837 as the home of the George Dyer family. In 1977 it was restored by the Carolina Foothills Garden Club and now houses The Metropolitan Arts Council and the Greenville Artists Guild Gallery.

Around the Town Homes Tour

Serves 8

Japanese Chicken Salad
Congealed Mandarin Orange Salad
Broiled Artichoke Rounds
Best Ever Pound Cake
Pineapple Dessert Sauce

Japanese Chicken Salad

6 chicken breast halves
Salt and pepper
1 small head of iceberg lettuce
3 stalks celery, chopped
3 tablespoons sugar
1½ teaspoons salt
1½ teaspoons Accent
¾ cup salad oil

1½ tablespoons sesame oil
5 tablespoons vinegar
3 ounces Japanese rice sticks, fried
⅓ cup chopped cashew nuts, toasted
3 tablespoons sesame seeds, toasted

Season chicken breast halves with salt and pepper; wrap in aluminum foil and bake at 350° for 45 minutes. Remove foil. Let cool. Remove meat from bone and shred. Shred lettuce. Combine lettuce, celery and chicken and refrigerate for several hours. For dressing, combine sugar, salt, Accent, oils and vinegar and store in refrigerator until ready to use. Shortly before serving time, fry rice sticks according to package directions and drain. When ready to serve, toss refrigerated lettuce mixture with nuts, seeds and dressing. Top salad with fried rice sticks. Serve immediately. Serves 8.

Congealed Mandarin Orange Salad

1 3-ounce package orange Jello
1 cup hot tea
1 cup crushed pineapple, drained
1 11-ounce can mandarin oranges
1 cup reserved fruit juices

1 cup water chestnuts, chopped
¼ cup whipping cream
½ cup mayonnaise
¼ teaspoon mace
Grated rind of two oranges
1 teaspoon sugar

Dissolve Jello in hot tea. Drain pineapple and oranges, reserving juices. Add pineapple, oranges, juices and water chestnuts to Jello. Pour mixture into a 4-cup salad mold and chill until set, approximately 3 hours. To prepare dressing, blend whipping cream, mayonnaise, mace, grated rind and sugar and spoon over individual salad servings. Serves 8.

Broiled Artichoke Rounds

2 14-ounce cans artichoke
  hearts
1 cup mayonnaise

1 cup grated Parmesan cheese
6 English muffins, split
Paprika

Drain artichokes and coarsely chop. Stir in mayonnaise and Parmesan cheese. Mound cheese mixture on muffin halves and spread evenly. Sprinkle with paprika. Place muffin halves on cookie sheet and broil until lightly browned. Yield: 12 rounds.

Best Ever Pound Cake

1½ cups butter
3 cups sugar
6 eggs
3 cups plain flour

1 cup heavy cream
2 tablespoons lemon juice
2 teaspoons vanilla extract
2 teaspoons almond extract

Preheat oven to 350°. Cream butter and sugar until light and fluffy. Add eggs 1 at a time, beating thoroughly after each addition. Sift flour 3 times. Add flour and cream alternately to creamed mixture. Add lemon juice, vanilla and almond extract; beat thoroughly. Pour batter into greased and floured 10-inch tube pan. Bake 1 hour and 45 minutes to 2 hours. Allow to cool in pan on wire rack. Remove cake from pan. Top each slice with Pineapple Dessert Sauce and garnish serving with whole fresh strawberries, if desired. Serves 20-24.

Pineapple Dessert Sauce

¾ cup sugar
1 tablespoon plain flour
2 eggs, beaten
1 cup pineapple juice

3 tablespoons butter
1 cup whipping cream
1 tablespoon powdered sugar

Blend sugar and flour and place in top of double boiler. Add beaten eggs, pineapple juice and butter. Cook, stirring constantly, until mixture is thick. Remove from heat, let cool. In a bowl, combine whipping cream and sugar; beat mixture until soft peaks are formed. Fold whipped cream into cooled pineapple sauce. Refrigerate for 24 hours. Stir before serving. This sauce is also delicious served over fresh fruits in season. Yield: approximately 4 cups.

From downtown condominiums and historic homes to spacious suburban neighborhoods, Greenville homes reflect converging tastes and lifestyles, a blend of the old and the new. Annually, there are tours of homes and gardens sponsored by various organizations. These tours have become a wonderful way to sample the variety of Greenville, while raising proceeds to benefit worthwhile charities.

Mom's Back-to-School Celebration

Serves 8

Mulled Citrus Punch
Cheesy Chicken Chowder
Fruit Salad in Cream
Poppy Seed Bread Sticks
Chocolate Bavarian

Mulled Citrus Punch

¼ cup sugar	2 2-inch sticks cinnamon
¼ cup water	1 quart orange juice
6 whole cloves	2 cups apple cider

Make a syrup of the first 4 ingredients by simmering 10 minutes. Remove spices. Add orange juice and cider. Float clove-spiked oranges in punch for additional flavor. Yield: 48 ounces.

Cheesy Chicken Chowder

8 tablespoons butter	1 teaspoon Worcestershire sauce
2 cups shredded carrots	
½ cup chopped onion	8 ounces cheddar cheese, shredded
½ cup flour	
3 cups chicken broth	2 tablespoons white wine, optional
4 cups milk	
2 cups diced cooked chicken	1 teaspoon salt
1 cup corn, fresh or frozen	½ teaspoon pepper

Melt butter in a skillet. Add carrots and onion and saute until tender. Blend in flour. Then add broth and milk. Cook and stir until thick and smooth. Add remaining ingredients and stir until cheese is melted. Serves 8.

Fruit Salad in Cream

1 tablespoon butter
2 tablespoons lemon juice
1 egg yolk, slightly beaten
1 cup whipping cream
2 tablespoons powdered sugar
1 teaspoon vanilla extract
1 16-ounce can pineapple
  chunks

3 oranges, peeled and sectioned
2 bananas, sliced
1 cup white grapes, halved
3 cups miniature marshmallows
1 kiwi, peeled and sliced
Lettuce

Mix butter, lemon juice and egg yolk together and cook over low heat until thick. Let mixture cool. Whip cream with powdered sugar and vanilla. Fold into lemon juice mixture. Drain pineapple and add to whipped cream dressing along with other fruits and marshmallows just before serving. Serve on lettuce and garnish with kiwi. Serves 8.

Poppy Seed Bread Sticks

2 cups plain flour
½ teaspoon salt
1 teaspoon baking soda
⅓ cup shortening

¼ cup white vinegar
½ cup milk
Poppy seeds

Sift dry ingredients into a large bowl. Cut shortening into mixture. Mix in vinegar. Divide dough into 16 balls. Roll each ball into 6-inch cylinder. Place on a lightly greased baking sheet 2 inches apart. Brush with milk; sprinkle with poppy seeds. Bake at 450° for 10-12 minutes. Yield: 16 sticks.

Chocolate Bavarian

½ cup cold milk
2 envelopes unflavored gelatin
12 ounces semi-sweet chocolate
  chips
1 cup hot milk
1 cup whipping cream

2 eggs
⅓ cup sugar
2 tablespoons rum
1 cup ice cubes
Whipped cream, optional
Chocolate shavings, optional

Pour milk into blender and sprinkle with gelatin. Let stand until gelatin granules are moistened. Add chocolate chips and hot milk. Cover and blend at low speed for 2 minutes or until chocolate is melted and gelatin is dissolved. Stop blender. Add whipping cream, eggs, sugar and rum; cover and process at high speed until well blended. With blender still running, remove center cap of lid and add ice cubes one at a time; blend until ice melts. Pour immediately into individual dessert dishes. Chill 30 minutes or until set. Garnish with whipped cream and chocolate shavings, if desired. Serves 8-10.

Spring Luncheon on the Terrace

Serves 8

Strawberry Slush
Golden Italian Ham Stacks
Crunchy Garden Peas
Cran-Orange Salad
Banana Split Pie

Strawberry Slush

12 ice cubes
2 cups fresh strawberries
1 6-ounce can frozen orange
   juice

3 teaspoons sugar
White wine to taste, optional

Wash and hull strawberries, reserving 8 berries for garnish. In a blender or food processor, crush ice. Add strawberries, orange juice concentrate, sugar and white wine, blending after each addition until slush consistency. Pour into chilled wine glasses, top with a fresh strawberry and serve. Yield: 8 4-ounce servings.

Golden Italian Ham Stacks

8-ounces cream cheese,
   softened
½ cup butter, softened
½ cup grated Parmesan cheese
1 teaspoon paprika

½ teaspoon oregano
½ teaspoon garlic powder
4 English muffins, split
1 pound baked ham, shaved
8 tomato slices

Combine cream cheese and butter; stir until smooth. Stir in Parmesan cheese, paprika, oregano and garlic powder. Spread ⅔ mixture evenly over cut surface of English muffins; top each with shaved ham and a tomato slice. Top each tomato slice with dollop of remaining cheese mixture. Place on baking sheet and broil until golden brown. Serve hot. Yield: 8 muffin halves.

Crunchy Garden Peas

1 17-ounce can petite garden
   peas
1 4-ounce jar diced pimento
1 cup grated sharp cheddar
   cheese
½ cup finely chopped celery
1 small onion, finely chopped

1 2-ounce package slivered
   almonds
2 tablespoons of commercial
   cole slaw dressing or
   mayonnaise
Lettuce leaves

continued

Drain peas and pimentos. In a medium bowl, combine all ingredients except cole slaw dressing and lettuce leaves. Toss ingredients with dressing. If available, Marsetti Slaw dressing is preferred. Cover and chill at least one hour before serving. Serves 8

Cran-Orange Salad

2 3½-ounce packages lemon
  Jello
2 cups boiling water
1 16-ounce can whole berry
  cranberry sauce
1 15½-ounce can crushed
  pineapple

Grated rind of 1 orange
2 oranges, peeled and sectioned
½ cup pecans
1 cup cottage cheese, optional

Dissolve Jello in boiling water. Chill until slightly thickened in a 8-inch square dish. Add cranberry sauce, pineapple, orange rind and orange sections. Fold in pecans. Chill until firm. Cut into 8 portions and serve on lettuce leaves. Serves 8.

Banana Split Pie

1 cup vanilla wafer crumbs
½ cup butter, melted
½ cup chopped pecans
6 ounces semi-sweet chocolate
  chips
1 cup miniature marshmallows
¼ cup milk
2 medium bananas

1 3-ounce package instant
  vanilla pudding
1½ cups milk
½ cup whipping cream, whipped
2 cups miniature marshmallows
½ cup whipping cream, whipped
½ cup crushed pecans

In a 9-inch pie pan, combine vanilla wafer crumbs, melted butter and pecans to form crust. Bake at 375° for 5 minutes. Let cool. In a small sauce pan, melt chocolate chips, 1 cup of miniature marshmallows and milk. Pour chocolate mixture into crust and chill. Slice bananas into rounds and arrange over chocolate layer. Stir 1½ cups milk into pudding. Blend until thickened. Fold ½ cup whipping cream whipped and 2 cups marshmallows into pudding mixture and layer over bananas. Top with remaining ½ cup whipped cream; sprinkle pie with crushed pecans. Refrigerate until ready to serve. Serves 8.

A luncheon on the terrace in Greenville is an outing that could possibly be held during any season of the year, not just the spring. Greenville's moderate climate is one of the delightful characteristics that has long attracted people to the area.

Down South Sunday Luncheon

Serves 8

Glazed Ham Loaf
Asparagus and Peas Almondine
Pineapple Cheese Strata
Sweet Potato Muffins
Chocolate Coconut Chess Pie

Glazed Ham Loaf

1 egg	¼ cup vinegar
Milk	1 teaspoon dry mustard
1 pound pre-cooked ground ham	½ cup vinegar
½ pound raw ground pork	½ cup sugar
2 cups Rice Krispies	2 eggs
1 cup brown sugar	⅛ teaspoon salt
1 cup water	2 teaspoons butter

Preheat oven to 350°. Beat egg in a measuring cup and add enough milk to make one cup of liquid. Combine ham, pork and Rice Krispies and shape into a loaf. Put in loaf pan. Prepare glaze by mixing brown sugar, water and vinegar. Baste loaf with glaze and place in oven. Cook for 1 hour and 35 minutes. Baste frequently during cooking. Pour remaining glaze over loaf during the last 30 minutes of cooking. To prepare mustard sauce, combine mustard, ½ cup vinegar, sugar, 2 eggs and salt in saucepan and boil until thickened. Remove from heat and cool slightly. Add butter and stir until smooth. To serve, remove ham loaf to serving platter and serve mustard sauce on the side. Serves 8.

Asparagus and Peas Almondine

2 6-ounce cans asparagus	1 cup slivered almonds, toasted
2 17-ounce cans early peas	2 10¾-ounce cans cream of
2 8-ounce cans sliced	chicken soup
mushrooms	Salt and pepper to taste
2 small onions	1 teaspoon Worcestershire
1 cup butter	sauce
8 hard-cooked eggs, chopped	Dry bread crumbs

Drain all vegetables. Saute onion in butter. Mix all ingredients together except bread crumbs. Pour into 9x13-inch glass casserole. Before baking, top with bread crumbs. Bake at 350° for 30 minutes. Serves 12.

Pineapple Cheese Strata

40 ounces unsweetened pineapple	2 cups grated cheddar cheese
½ cup sugar	¾ cup butter
¼ cup flour	8 ounces Ritz crackers

Drain pineapple and place in 3-quart casserole. Mix sugar, flour and cheese and pour over pineapple. Melt butter. Crush crackers and mix with butter. Spread on top of pineapple mixture. Bake at 350° for 25 minutes. Serves 8.

Sweet Potato Muffins

½ cup butter	¼ teaspoon salt
1¼ cups sugar	1 teaspoon cinnamon
2 eggs	¼ teaspoon nutmeg
1¼ cups mashed sweet potatoes	1 cup milk
1½ cups plain flour	¼ cup chopped walnuts
2 teaspoons baking powder	½ cup raisins, chopped

Preheat oven to 400°. Grease muffin tins. Cream butter and sugar. Add eggs and mix well. Blend in sweet potatoes. Sift flour with baking powder, salt, cinnamon and nutmeg. Add alternately with milk. Do not overmix. Fold in nuts and raisins. Fill greased muffin tins ⅔ full. Bake at 400° for 25 minutes. Sweet potato muffins can be frozen and reheated. Yield: 24 muffins.

Chocolate Coconut Chess Pie

½ cup butter	1 cup coconut
4 cups sugar	1 cup chopped pecans
5 eggs	3 pie crusts, unbaked
½ cup cocoa	Whipped cream or whipped
1 12-ounce can evaporated milk	topping, optional
1 tablespoon vanilla extract	

Cream butter and sugar. Add remaining ingredients and mix thoroughly. Pour into pie crusts. Bake at 350° for 50 minutes. Garnish with whipped cream or topping, if desired. Yield: 3 pies, 2 for lunch and 1 for a friend.

Down South Sundays have centered around churches for many generations. Among the noteworthy and historic churches in the area are Christ Church, McBee Chapel and Fairview Presbyterian. Christ Church stands in downtown Greenville as an example of Gothic Revival architecture. While the building was begun in 1857, its congregation was organized in 1820 as St. James Episcopal Mission. McBee Chapel, located just outside of Greenville in Conestee, is one of the few remaining octagonal churches in America. It was built in 1841 near the site of one of Vardry McBee's early mills. Just off of U.S. Highway 276 on Fairview Road stands Fairview Presbyterian Church. Founded in 1786 and built in 1857 it houses old family pews and a slave gallery.

Before the Matinee

Serves 8

Bombay Chicken
Curried Rice
Pickled Asparagus
Sour Cream Gems
Luscious Lemon Pie

Bombay Chicken

8	chicken breast halves	2	tablespoons soy sauce
	Salt and paprika	4	tablespoons cooking oil
	Flour	1	teaspoon ginger
4	tablespoons cooking oil	4	teaspoons sesame seeds
1	cup sherry	8	peach halves
4	tablespoons brown sugar		

Rinse and dry chicken pieces. Season with salt and paprika, sprinkle with flour. Brown on both sides in hot oil. Remove pieces to large 9x13-inch baking pan. Combine sherry, brown sugar, soy sauce, oil, ginger and sesame seeds. Pour over chicken. Cover pan with aluminum foil. Bake at 375° for 45 minutes or until tender. To serve arrange chicken on platter and garnish with peaches. Serves 8.

Curried Rice

1⅓	cups raw rice	1	tablespoon wine vinegar
½	tablespoon curry powder	⅓	cup slivered almonds, toasted
3	tablespoons onion, finely chopped	1	cup celery, finely chopped
2	tablespoons butter or margarine	⅓	cup raisins, chopped
1	teaspoon salt	1	cup green peas, cooked
		¼	cup mayonnaise

Prepare rice according to package directions. Cook curry powder and onion in butter until onion is soft but not brown. Add to hot rice next 5 ingredients. Chill 3 hours. Add peas and mayonnaise. Pack in individual molds. Serves 8.

Pickled Asparagus

2 15-ounce cans asparagus
   spears
½ cup asparagus juice
1 cup vinegar
½ cup sugar
2 sticks cinnamon

1 teaspoon salt
6 whole cloves
½ teaspoon celery seed
   Lettuce leaves
   Pimento strips

Boil together all ingredients, excluding asparagus spears, lettuce and pimento, for 2 minutes. Place drained asparagus spears in a loaf-size pan. Pour boiled ingredients over asparagus. Refrigerate for 3 hours. Serve on lettuce leaf garnished with pimento strips. Serves 8.

Sour Cream Gems

2 cups unsifted self-rising flour
1 cup butter, softened

1 cup sour cream

Cut flour and butter together with a fork. Add sour cream, and stir until moistened. Spoon into greased miniature muffin tins and bake at 350° for 20-25 minutes. Yield: 24 miniature muffins.

Luscious Lemon Pie

1 9-inch pie shell, baked
1 cup sugar
3 tablespoons cornstarch
¼ cup butter
1 tablespoon grated lemon rind
½ cup lemon juice
3 egg yolks, unbeaten

1 cup milk
1 cup sour cream
1 cup whipping cream, whipped
2 tablespoons powdered sugar
2 tablespoons chopped nuts,
   optional

Combine sugar and cornstarch in saucepan. Add butter, lemon rind, lemon juice, and egg yolks. Stir in milk gradually, mixing well. Bring to boil over medium heat, stirring until thick. Cool. Fold in sour cream. Pour into pie shell and chill for at least 2 hours. Top with whipped cream sweetened with sugar. Garnish with chopped nuts, if desired. Serves 8.

If the Sugar Plum Fairy inspires every young ballet dancer, so will the programs and professional direction of the three civic ballet companies that call Greenville home. All present programs throughout the year, with two of the companies staging "The Nutcracker" during the holiday season. Before the matinee performance starring your favorite ballerina, serve this delightful luncheon to family or friends.

Parking Lot Picnic

Serves 8

Chestnut Dip
Barbecued Turkey Breast
Dublin Potato Salad
Marinated Vegetable Medley
Milky Way Cake

Chestnut Dip

1 8-ounce can water chestnuts, drained and chopped
½ cup parsley, chopped
2 green onions, chopped
1 cup sour cream
1 cup mayonnaise
2 teaspoons Tabasco sauce
2 teaspoons soy sauce

Mix together all ingredients and chill. Serve as a dip with raw vegetables or chips. Yield: 2 cups.

Barbecued Turkey Breast

8 pound turkey breast
1½ cups chili sauce
4½ cups hickory smoked barbecue sauce
Salt
Pepper

Salt and pepper turkey and place in roasting pan. In bowl mix chili sauce and barbecue sauce; baste turkey with sauce. Cover turkey with foil and bake at 200° for 4 hours. Then baste again and continue cooking covered for an additional 4 hours. Remove foil and baste turkey. Cook uncovered for 45 minutes (glaze will appear burned). Let turkey stand for about 30 minutes before slicing. Mix turkey drippings with remaining sauce to serve over turkey on sandwich buns. Serves 8-10.

Dublin Potato Salad

2 tablespoons vinegar
1 teaspoon celery seed
1 teaspoon mustard seed
3 large potatoes, cubed
2 teaspoons sugar
½ teaspoon salt
3 cups finely shredded cabbage
12 ounces corned beef, cubed
¼ cup finely chopped dill pickles
¼ cup diced green onion
Dressing:
1 cup mayonnaise
¼ cup milk
½ teaspoon salt

continued

Combine vinegar, celery seed and mustard seed; set aside. Cook potatoes and drain. While potato cubes are still warm, drizzle with vinegar mixture. Sprinkle with sugar and salt; chill thoroughly. Add cabbage, corned beef, pickle and onion. Mix dressing ingredients and pour over salad; toss lightly. Can be made night before serving. Serves 8.

Marinated Vegetable Medley

1 16-ounce can early garden peas	1 2-ounce jar chopped pimento
1 12-ounce can shoe peg corn	½ cup vegetable oil
2 1-pound cans French green beans	½ cup wine vinegar
1 large onion, chopped	¾ cup sugar
1 cup finely chopped celery	1 teaspoon salt
1 1-pound can lima beans	½ teaspoon pepper
	Cayenne pepper to taste

Drain canned vegetables. In a large bowl, mix drained vegetables with onion, celery and pimento. In a saucepan, combine oil, wine vinegar, sugar, salt, pepper and cayenne pepper and bring to a boil. Pour dressing over vegetables and marinate in refrigerator overnight. Marinated vegetables will keep in refrigerator for up to 2 weeks. Serves 10-12.

Milky Way Cake

6 2.1-ounce Milky Way bars	½ teaspoon baking soda
1 cup butter	1¼ cups buttermilk
2 cups sugar	1 teaspoon vanilla
4 eggs	2 cups chopped nuts
2½ cups sifted plain flour	

Combine Milky Way bars with ½ cup butter in a saucepan and melt over low heat. While candy is melting, cream ½ cup butter and sugar until light and fluffy. Add eggs, 1 at a time, beating well after each addition. Add flour and baking soda, alternately with buttermilk. Stir until smooth. Add melted candy, mixing well. Stir in vanilla and nuts. Pour batter into greased and floured Bundt pan. Bake at 350° for 1 hour and 20 minutes. Cool and remove from pan. Serves 20-24.

From football games to steeplechase horse races, this menu is an ideal outdoor tailgate. The entire picnic can be served buffet style from the tailgate or portable table or packed in small peach baskets for individual servings.

Children's Picnic in the Park

Serves 8

Cranapple Fizz
Mini-Subs
Stuffed Apples
Grape Animal Chewies
Triple Goodness
Hidden Treasure Pops

Cranapple Fizz

1 quart cranapple juice, chilled   *1 quart Sprite, chilled*

When ready to serve, mix equal parts of cranapple juice and Sprite.
Yield: 8 cups.

Mini-Subs

8 hot dog buns, split   *8 bologna slices*
Mustard   *Tomatoes, sliced*
Mayonnaise   *Shredded lettuce*
8 American cheese slices   *Salt and pepper to taste*
8 ham slices

Spread a thin layer of mustard and mayonnaise on the buns. Layer meats,
cheese, tomato and lettuce. Sprinkle with salt and pepper. Cut sandwich in
half and enclose in plastic wrap. Secure each half with a decorative pick.
Yield: 8 sandwiches.

Stuffed Apples

8 small apples   *½ cup granola*
3 ounces cream cheese,
softened

Core apples. Mix cream cheese with granola. Stuff apples with creamed
mixture. Enclose in plastic wrap and pack in lunch pail. Yield: 8 apples.

Grape Animal Chewies

12 ounces frozen grape juice   1½ cups water
3 envelopes unflavored gelatin

Thaw grape juice. Soften gelatin in the grape juice. Boil water; add gelatin mixture and stir until gelatin is dissolved. Remove from heat and pour into a lightly greased 9x13x2-inch pan and chill. When gelatin is firm, cut into animal shapes with cookie cutters. Refrigerate in a covered container. This concentrated gelatin can go unrefrigerated for 4 hours. Wrap individual "animals" in plastic wrap and add to lunch pail right before party time. Serves 8.

Triple Goodness

6 ounces butterscotch morsels   1½ cups salted peanuts
1½ cups golden raisins

Mix ingredients together. Package in individual plastic bags with small toy surprise. Serves 8.

Hidden Treasure Pops

½ cup sugar   1½ cups plain flour
½ cup brown sugar, firmly   ½ teaspoon baking powder
    packed   ½ teaspoon baking soda
½ cup margarine, softened   ¼ teaspoon salt
½ cup peanut butter   10 wooden sticks
1 teaspoon vanilla extract   10 Milky Way fun size candy bars
1 egg

In large bowl, combine sugar, brown sugar, margarine, peanut butter, vanilla and egg; beat well. Add flour, baking powder, baking soda and salt; mix well. Securely insert a wooden pick into small end of each candy bar forming a lollipop. Shape about ⅓ cup dough smoothly around each candy bar, making sure bar is completely covered. Place 4 inches apart on ungreased cookie sheets. Bake at 375° for 13-16 minutes or until golden brown. Cool 10 minutes and remove from cookie sheet. Cool completely and wrap each cookie in plastic wrap. Secure plastic wrap with a ribbon or tie. Yield: 10 pops.

This children's picnic menu can be packed into individual sandpails which may be used as party favors. Cover top of packed pail with a party napkin and let each child carry his own lunch.

River Place Picnic

Serves 8

Mother Rutledge's Boiled Peanuts
Parmesan Chicken Fingers
Curried Artichoke Rice
Broccoli-Cauliflower Salad
Crunchy Ham Pockets
Dilly Deviled Eggs
Orange Slice Cookies
Sinful German Chocolate Squares

Mother Rutledge's Boiled Peanuts

1 pound green peanuts   *½ cup salt*

Fill a 5-quart Dutch oven or large pan with water. Add green peanuts and salt. Boil 1½ hours. Let stand in water 3 hours. Drain. Serves 20.

Parmesan Chicken Fingers

8 boneless chicken breast halves
2 cups dry bread crumbs
¾ cup grated Parmesan cheese
1 teaspoon salt

½ teaspoon pepper
¼ cup chopped fresh parsley
2 garlic cloves, chopped
1 cup butter, melted

Remove skin and cut each chicken breast into 3-4 fingers. In large bowl combine bread crumbs, cheese, salt, pepper and parsley. Saute garlic in butter. Remove from heat; add chicken fingers and let sit for 3 minutes. Dip chicken in bread crumbs and place in a 9x13x2-inch baking dish. Top fingers with more bread crumbs and pour remaining butter over all. Bake at 400° for 18-20 minutes. Cool slightly and cover loosely with foil. Refrigerate until well-chilled and transport in cooler. Yield: 24 chicken fingers.

Curried Artichoke Rice

1 7-ounce package yellow rice mix
½ cup prepared garlic dressing
½ cup mayonnaise
2 14-ounce cans artichoke hearts, drained and coarsely chopped

6 spring onions with tops, sliced
1 medium green pepper, chopped
½ cup sliced green olives
Salt and pepper to taste
½ teaspoon curry powder

continued

Prepare rice according to package directions. Cool. Blend garlic dressing and mayonnaise. Pour over artichoke hearts. Mix cooled rice with artichoke mixture and toss. Add green onions, green pepper and olives. Season to taste with salt, pepper and curry powder, if desired. Garnish with cherry tomatoes. Serves 8.

Broccoli-Cauliflower Salad

1 head broccoli
½ head cauliflower
1 small purple onion, chopped fine
8 slices bacon, fried and crumbled

1 cup grated sharp cheddar cheese
½ cup mayonnaise
2 tablespoons sugar
1 tablespoon red wine vinegar

Wash broccoli and cauliflower and cut into small flowerettes. In large bowl, mix broccoli, cauliflower, onion and cheese. Blend mayonnaise, sugar and vinegar. Pour over broccoli-cauliflower mixture and toss until all ingredients are well coated. Refrigerate for at least 1 hour. Right before serving, add crumbled bacon and toss well. Serves 8.

Crunchy Ham Pockets

2 cups cooked diced ham
1 cup chopped celery
⅓ cup chopped green pepper
3 tablespoons chopped spring onion
½ cup mayonnaise

1 tablespoon stone ground mustard
1 teaspoon salt
½ teaspoon pepper
Pita bread halves

Mix all ingredients together, except bread, and chill. Place salad in bowl on plate surrounded by lettuce leaves. To serve, place lettuce leaf in pita and fill with ham salad. Yield: 3 cups ham salad.

Dilly Deviled Eggs

12 hard-cooked eggs
5 tablespoons mayonnaise
4 teaspoons vinegar
½ teaspoon dry mustard

¼ teaspoon black pepper
1 teaspoon dill
Salt to taste
Paprika

Halve eggs. Mash yolks and combine with remaining ingredients except paprika until blended. Stuff eggs with yolk mixture and sprinkle with paprika. Yield: 24 deviled eggs.

Orange Slice Cookies

1 cup sugar
1 cup brown sugar, firmly packed
1 cup shortening
2 eggs
1 teaspoon vanilla extract
2 cups plain flour

1 teaspoon baking powder
1 teaspoon baking soda
½ teaspoon salt
2 cups quick cooking rolled oats
1 cup flaked coconut
10 slices of jellied orange candy

In a large mixing bowl, cream sugars and shortening until fluffy. Add eggs and vanilla and blend well. Combine flour, baking powder, baking soda and salt and gradually blend into creamed sugar. Stir into batter the oats and the coconut. Cut the slices of orange candy into small pieces. HINT: Keep your knife and fingers moist while cutting the candy to keep the candy from sticking to your fingers and knife. Stir the candy into the batter. Use 1 tablespoon of batter and form a loose ball for each cookie. Place balls on a greased cookie sheet and bake for 8 to 10 minutes in preheated 350° oven. Yield: 6 dozen.

Sinful German Chocolate Squares

1 14-ounce bag of caramel candies
⅔ cup evaporated milk, divided
1 18½ ounce package German chocolate cake mix

¾ cup of softened butter
1 cup chopped pecans
6 ounces semi-sweet chocolate chips

Preheat oven to 350°. Combine caramels and ⅓ cup of evaporated milk in top of double boiler. Heat, stirring constantly, until caramels are completely melted. Remove from heat and set aside. Combine cake mix, remaining ⅓ cup of evaporated milk and butter. Beat with electric mixer until mixture holds together. Stir in nuts. Press half of mixture into well-greased 9x13-baking pan. Bake for 6 minutes. Sprinkle chocolate chips over crust. Cover evenly with caramel mixture. Crumble remaining cake mixture on top of caramel layer. Bake 17-20 minutes. Cool. Chill for 30 minutes before cutting into small squares. Yield: 5 dozen.

Located in the heart of Greenville is Reedy River Falls Historic Park, the site of Greenville's first permanent settlement in the late 1760's. Today the lovely park and falls are the setting for the River Place Festival, a semi-annual spring arts and leisure festival sponsored by the Metropolitan Arts Council.

Ladies' Afternoon Tea

Serves 25

Charleston Shrimp Sandwich
Curried Chicken Bites
Bacon-Marmalade Rounds
Lemon Muffins
Chocolate Truffles
Candied Walnuts
Party Cheesecakes
Apricot Spice Cake
Citrus Sherbert Punch

Charleston Shrimp Sandwich

1 pound fresh cooked shrimp	1/8 teaspoon garlic salt
8 ounces cream cheese	1/8 teaspoon mace
1/4 teaspoon onion powder	Mayonnaise
1 tablespoon lemon juice	Whole wheat bread

Grind shrimp in food processor. Mix in all other ingredients and fold in enough mayonnaise to make a paste. Spread on whole wheat bread and cut diagonally into 4 triangles. Yield: 2½ cups of spread.

Curried Chicken Bites

4 ounces cream cheese	1 tablespoon chutney, chopped
2 tablespoons mayonnaise	1/2 teaspoon salt
1 cup cooked chopped chicken breasts	1 teaspoon curry powder
1 cup blanched almonds, chopped	1 cup grated coconut

Beat together cream cheese and mayonnaise. Add chicken, almonds, chutney, salt, and curry powder. Shape into walnut sized balls. Roll in grated coconut. Chill. Yield: 34.

Bacon-Marmalade Rounds

1 pound cheddar cheese, grated	Melba rounds
8 ounces cream cheese	1/2 pound cooked bacon, crumbled
3 egg yolks	
1/2 cup orange marmalade	

Mix cheeses with egg yolks. Blend in marmalade. Spread mixture on melba rounds. Top with bacon. Broil until hot and bubbly. Yield: 40.

Lemon Muffins

½ cup sugar
½ cup butter
2 egg yolks
Grated rind and juice
of 1 lemon

1 cup plain flour
1 teaspoon baking powder
2 egg whites, stiffly beaten

Cream sugar and butter together; mix next 4 ingredients in order with the creamed mixture. Fold in egg whites last. Fill greased mini-muffin tins and bake 15 minutes at 350°. Roll or dip in powdered sugar. Yield: 30 mini-muffins.

Chocolate Truffles

1⅔ cups heavy cream
½ cup unsalted butter
1 pound fine grade semi-sweet
chocolate

2 tablespoons Grand Marnier
Dutch process cocoa or
powdered sugar

Melt butter and cream over medium heat in heavy saucepan, stirring with a rubber spatula. Raise the heat and bring cream just to a boil. Take it off the heat and add the chocolate and stir until melted. Stir until mixture cools and thickens. Stir in Grand Marnier and cover; place in refrigerator. Allow to thicken for 2-3 hours, stirring several times as it cools. After mixture has hardened, form truffles by scooping portions with a small spoon. Work quickly and dust your hands with cocoa or powdered sugar, and roll in cocoa or sugar. These may also be cut into tiny squares and powdered with cocoa or sugar. Will keep stored in refrigerator or freezer indefinitely. May be arranged on a platter or tray in the form of a grape cluster with chocolate leaves. These make a beautiful gift in decorative tins in candy papers. Yield: 50.

Candied Walnuts

1½ cups sugar
½ cup water
¼ cup light corn syrup

1 teaspoon vanilla extract
4 cups shelled whole walnuts

Mix sugar, water and light corn syrup in saucepan. Heat to 240° with candy thermometer to soft ball stage. Remove from heat and add vanilla. Stir in walnuts and mix until they are coated. Pour onto wax paper to cool. Break apart. Yield: 1 pound candy.

Party Cheesecakes

2½ cups graham cracker crumbs
6 tablespoons sugar
⅔ cup butter, melted
24 ounces cream cheese
1½ cups sugar

4 eggs
4 tablespoons vanilla extract
16 ounces sour cream
  Strawberry halves

To make crust, combine crumbs and 6 tablespoons of sugar. Stir in butter until thoroughly blended. Press mixture firmly into 13x9x2-inch pan. Bake at 350° for 8 minutes; cool. Mix remaining ingredients except sour cream and strawberries, blending until smooth. Pour filling into cooled crust and bake at 350° for 30 minutes. Cool about 3 minutes then spread with sour cream. Refrigerate overnight. Cut in 1-inch squares and top with strawberry half. Yield: 96.

Apricot Spice Cake

1 cup vegetable oil
2 cups sugar
2 cups self-rising flour
4 eggs
1 teaspoon cinnamon

1 cup nuts, optional
1 teaspoon vanilla extract
1 teaspoon cloves
2 small jars apricot baby food

Blend oil, sugar and flour. Add eggs, one at a time. Add remaining ingredients and beat. Pour in greased and floured tube or Bundt pan. Bake at 325° for 50-60 minutes. Serves 20-24.

Citrus Sherbert Punch

1 6-ounce can frozen orange
  juice
1 6-ounce can frozen lemonade
1 6-ounce can frozen limeade

4 cups very cold water
1 quart ginger ale, chilled
1 gallon pineapple sherbert

Let juices thaw about 30 minutes until slightly thawed. Mix juices, water and ginger ale in large container and refrigerate. When serving, place juice in punch bowl and float large scoops of sherbert on top. As sherbert melts, stir into punch. Make this right before serving so that the sherbert keeps it cold and you do not have to use ice. Serves 24.

This tea is a lovely way to honor a bride-to-be, debutante or welcome a new neighbor. For a special, delicious gift or favor, prepare Chocolate Truffles in advance and box attractively. Instead of using ice cubes to keep wine chilled, freeze clusters of red or green grapes and pour wine over in individual glasses.

NOTES

EVENING MEN

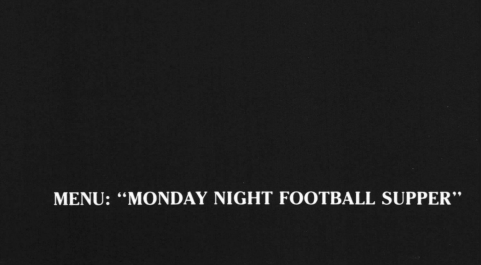

MENU: "MONDAY NIGHT FOOTBALL SUPPER"

Uptown Down South

Serves 8

Crab Meat Imperials
Citrus Almond Salad
Honey-Orange Dressing
Veal Nicholas
Orzo with Onions and Parsley
Baby Carrots in Cream
Baked Fresh Asparagus
Raspberry Continental

Crab Meat Imperials

9 bread slices	1 cup grated cheddar cheese
1 7.5 ounce can flaked crab meat	1 cup mayonnaise
	1 teaspoon curry powder
1 small onion, finely minced	¼ teaspoon salt

Remove crust from bread and cut each slice into 4 squares. Mix remaining ingredients. Spread on bread and place on cookie sheet. Can be prepared to this point and frozen. To serve, broil until browned and bubbly. Yield: 36 appetizers.

Citrus Almond Salad

2 pink grapefruit	2½ ounces sliced almonds, toasted
4 oranges	
1 fresh pineapple	Bibb lettuce

Peel and section grapefruit and oranges. Cut pineapple into chunks. Mix fresh fruits and mound on top of Bibb lettuce. Serve topped with Honey-Orange dressing. Sprinkle with toasted almonds. Serves 8.

Honey-Orange Dressing

1 tablespoon frozen orange juice	⅛ teaspoon cinnamon
2 teaspoons honey	1 small banana, sliced
⅛ teaspoon ginger	8 ounces orange flavored yogurt

Combine first 5 ingredients in a food processor or blender; process until smooth. Place yogurt and mixture in a bowl and blend gently. Refrigerate. Yield: 1½ cups.

Veal Nicholas

1 boned 3-pound veal roast, tied at 2-inch intervals
11 tablespoons butter
1 carrot, chopped
1 onion, chopped
2 sprigs fresh parsley, chopped
1 bay leaf
1/3 cup white wine
2 tablespoons minced green onions
1/2 pound fresh mushrooms, minced

Salt and pepper to taste
1/4 cup white wine
3 tablespoons plain flour
2 cups milk, scalded
Salt and pepper to taste
Nutmeg to taste
2 egg yolks
1/2 cup grated Gruyere cheese
8 thin slices ham
8 thin slices Gruyere cheese

Place veal in 4 tablespoons melted butter in large roasting pan. Bake at 375° for 15 minutes, turning veal every 5 minutes. Remove veal from pan. In roasting pan make bed of carrot, onion, parsley and bay leaf. Place veal on top. Return to oven and bake for 15 minutes. Add 1/3 cup wine; bake 20 minutes or until juices run clear. Remove from oven and let veal rest 20 minutes. Prepare mushroom mixture by melting 4 tablespoons of butter in skillet. Add green onions and saute for 2 minutes. Stir in mushrooms, salt and pepper; cook until moisture evaporates. Add 1/4 cup wine; cook until liquid is reduced completely. Prepare cheese sauce by melting 3 tablespoons butter in pan. Add flour. Cook for 2 minutes, stirring constantly. Remove from heat; add milk and whisk until smooth. Stir in salt, pepper and nutmeg. Cook, stirring constantly, until thickened. Remove from heat; beat in egg yolks. Stir in 1/2 cup cheese. Cook until cheese melts. Cut veal into eight 1/2-inch slices. On an ovenproof platter place pieces of veal. On each veal slice, place 1/8 mushroom mixture, slice of ham, and slice of cheese. Cover with cheese sauce. When ready to serve, bake at 375° for 30 minutes. Place under broiler 3 minutes to brown. Serves 8.

Orzo with Onions and Parsley

3 quarts water
1 1/2 teaspoons salt
2 cups orzo

6 tablespoons butter
2 medium onions, chopped
2 tablespoons parsley

In a large pot bring salted water to a boil. Add orzo and cook for 12 minutes or just until tender. Drain. Melt butter and saute onions in skillet over medium heat for 5 minutes. Add orzo and parsley to the onions. Stir well and serve immediately. Serves 8.

Baby Carrots in Cream

2 pounds fingerling carrots
6 tablespoons butter
½ teaspoon salt
2 teaspoons sugar

2½ cups water
1 cup heavy cream
2 tablespoons dried parsley

Put the carrots, butter, salt, sugar and water in a saucepan. Cook, uncovered, over medium heat until carrots are tender and water has almost evaporated, about 15 minutes. Stir in cream and parsley. Cook gently for about 4-5 minutes until cream is warm. Serves 8.

Baked Fresh Asparagus

2 pounds fresh asparagus, trimmed

Salt and pepper to taste
10 tablespoons butter

Place asparagus in shallow baking dish. Sprinkle with salt and pepper and dot with 6 tablespoons butter. Cover with foil and bake at 300° for 30 minutes. Transfer asparagus to serving dish. Add remaining butter to pan juices. Season with salt and pepper and pour over asparagus. Serves 8.

Raspberry Continental

½ cup butter
1 cup sugar
1 egg
¼ cup milk
1 teaspoon vanilla extract
½ teaspoon salt
1¼ cups plain flour, sifted
¼ cup chopped almonds, toasted
½ cup butter

1½ cups powdered sugar, sifted
1 egg
¼ cup sugar
2 tablespoons cornstarch
1 10-ounce package frozen red raspberries
1 cup whipping cream
3 tablespoons powdered sugar
Sliced almonds, toasted

Cream ½ cup butter and sugar. Add egg, milk, vanilla and salt. Stir in flour and almonds. Pour into greased 8-inch square pan and bake at 350° for 30-35 minutes. Remove from pan and cool on rack. Slice cake in half horizontally. To prepare butter filling, cream ½ cup butter with powdered sugar. Add egg and beat until fluffy. To prepare raspberry filling, combine ¼ cup sugar and cornstarch in a saucepan over medium heat. Add the raspberries and cook, stirring constantly until thickened. Cool completely. To assemble dessert, spread bottom layer of cake with butter filling. Top with raspberry filling. Place remaining cake layer on raspberry filling. Whip cream with 3 tablespoons powdered sugar. Ice top and sides with whipped cream. Garnish with almonds. Chill for 4 hours before serving. Serves 8.

A Neighborly Welcome

Serves 6

Creamed Lettuce Soup
Company Cornish Hens
Easy Raisin Rice
Spinach-Artichoke Casserole
Heavenly Biscuits
Pumpkin Chiffon Pie

Creamed Lettuce Soup

1 head iceberg lettuce, chopped	1 bay leaf
5 tablespoons butter, divided	1¼ cups chicken broth
3 green onions, thinly sliced	2 egg yolks, beaten
1 medium onion, chopped	3 tablespoons plain flour
3 cups milk	Salt to taste
2 whole cloves	½ teaspoon lemon pepper
2 tablespoons chopped fresh parsley	Croutons

Blanch lettuce in boiling, salted water for 5 minutes and drain. In medium saucepan, melt 2 tablespoons butter. Add onions and saute until tender. Add milk, cloves, parsley and bay leaf. Over low heat, bring mixture to a boil. Remove from heat, drain and discard cloves and bay leaf, reserving liquid. In food processor or blender, process strained green onion, onion, parsley and lettuce with chicken broth until liquified. Into this mixture, stir egg yolks. In Dutch oven, melt remaining butter. Add flour, stirring constantly, for 2 minutes. Stir in reserved liquid, salt, lemon pepper and chicken broth mixture. Heat soup, stirring constantly, until thoroughly heated. Top with croutons. Serves 6.

Company Cornish Hens

4 1½-pound Cornish hens	6 tablespoons butter, melted
Garlic salt to taste	½ cup dry white wine
Salt and pepper to taste	8 ounces sour cream
1 medium onion, chopped	
8 ounces fresh mushrooms, sliced	

continued

Split hens lengthwise and sprinkle with seasonings. Place cut side down in a lightly greased 9x13-inch baking pan. Cover with aluminum foil; bake at 350° for 30 minutes. Remove foil and bake an additional 30 minutes. Saute onion and mushrooms in butter over medium heat for 5 minutes; stir in wine. Pour wine mixture over hens. Bake an additional 25 minutes or until juice runs clear when thigh is pierced with fork. Place hens on serving platter, reserving pan drippings. Whisk sour cream into pan drippings and pour over hens. Serves 6.

Easy Raisin Rice

1/4 cup butter
3 green onions with tops, chopped
1 10 1/2-ounce can chicken broth
1 1/4 cups water

1 cup uncooked long grain rice
1 cup golden raisins
1/4 cup finely chopped fresh parsley
1/2 cup shelled sunflower seeds

Saute onions in butter over medium heat until clear. Put onions in 2-quart baking dish; stir in remaining ingredients except seeds. Cover dish and bake at 350° for 45 minutes or until liquid is absorbed. Before serving, stir in seeds. Serves 6.

Spinach-Artichoke Casserole

2 10-ounce packages frozen chopped spinach
1 small onion, chopped
1 4-ounce can sliced mushrooms, drained
1/4 cup butter

1 14-ounce can artichoke hearts, drained
1 10 3/4-ounce can cream of mushroom soup
1 1 1/2-ounce can Parmesan cheese
Seasoned bread crumbs

Cook spinach according to package directions; drain. Saute onion and mushrooms in butter. Grease 9x13x2-inch baking dish. Chop artichoke hearts and layer in baking dish. Layer spinach over artichokes. Combine soup, cheese, onion, and mushrooms. Pour over spinach. Sprinkle top with seasoned bread crumbs. Bake at 350° for 20-30 minutes until browned and bubbly. Serves 6.

Heavenly Biscuits

1 package active dry yeast
2 tablespoons very warm water
5 cups plain flour
1 teaspoon soda
3 teaspoons baking powder

2 tablespoons sugar
1 1/2 teaspoons salt
1 cup shortening
2 cups buttermilk
2 tablespoons butter, melted

continued

Dissolve yeast in water. Sift all dry ingredients into large bowl. Cut in shortening with pastry blender. Add buttermilk, then dissolved yeast. Stir until thoroughly moistened. Turn onto floured surface and knead 1 minute. Roll dough to ½-inch thickness and cut with 2-inch biscuit cutter. Place on ungreased baking sheet and brush with melted butter. Bake at 400° for 12-15 minutes, or until lightly browned. Biscuits may be prepared ahead and frozen; then removed from freezer and allowed to reach room temperature before baking. Dough keeps several days refrigerated in plastic bag or covered bowl. Yield: 60 2-inch biscuits.

Pumpkin-Chiffon Pie

2 10-inch deep dish pie shells	5 eggs, separated
¾ cup milk	2 envelopes unflavored gelatin
1 1-pound can pumpkin	⅓ cup cold water
1½ cups brown sugar, firmly packed	1½ cups heavy cream
⅛ teaspoon salt	¾ teaspoon grated orange rind
1½ teaspoons ginger	⅓ cup sugar
1½ teaspoons cinnamon	1 cup heavy cream
⅔ teaspoon nutmeg	Powdered sugar
	Grated orange rind

Bake pie shells according to package directions. Heat milk in top of double boiler, with pumpkin, brown sugar, salt and spices. Beat egg yolks slightly. Add hot mixture to yolks gradually. Mix well and cook in double boiler until thickened, stirring constantly. Soften gelatin in cold water. Add to hot custard and stir until dissolved. Cool until it begins to thicken. Beat egg whites until stiff but not dry. Fold beaten egg whites into cooled custard. Chill, but do not allow to set. Beat 1½ cups cream until stiff. Fold in ¾ teaspoon of grated orange rind and ⅓ cup sugar. Fold into chilled pumpkin mixture. Chill until thick. Pour into pie shells. Chill until set. Beat remaining heavy cream, sweetened with powdered sugar. To serve, top each slice with dollop of whipped cream and sprinkle with orange rind. Yield: 2 pies — one for guests and 1 for keeps.

As Greenville's horizons have broadened, welcoming a neighbor sometimes means more than someone from out of state. Many international businessmen visit our area. When you are called upon to entertain foreign colleagues, treat them to this truly American meal featuring Cornish hens and pumpkin pie.

Dinner Party on Paris Mountain

Serves 8

Tomato Bisque
Roast Pork Au Vin Blanc
Noodles with Poppy Seeds
Brown Sugared Apricots
Broccoli Stuffed Squash
Hearty Bran Biscuits
Upside Down Lemon Meringue

Tomato Bisque

¾ cup butter
2 tablespoons olive oil
1 large onion, thinly sliced
½ teaspoon dried thyme
¾ teaspoon salt
½ teaspoon pepper
3 fresh ripe tomatoes

3 tablespoons tomato paste
¼ cup plain flour
3¾ cups chicken broth
1 teaspoon sugar
1 cup heavy cream
Fresh dill

Heat ½ cup butter and oil together in Dutch oven. Add onion, thyme, salt and pepper. Cook until onion is wilted. Add tomatoes and tomato paste; stir to blend. Simmer for 10 minutes. Put flour in small bowl. Add 5 tablespoons broth to flour; blend well. Stir flour paste into tomato mixture. Add remaining broth. Simmer for 30 minutes, stirring frequently. Remove from heat and cool. Pour cooled mixture into blender or processor; blend well. Strain mixture. Add sugar and cream to strained mixture and simmer for 5 minutes. Add remaining butter. May be served hot or cold. If serving cold, sprinkle with fresh dill. Serves 8.

Roast Pork Au Vin Blanc

1 5-pound pork loin roast
½ large lemon
1 garlic clove, halved
Marjoram
Salt and pepper to taste

⅓ cup dry white wine
¾ cup sour cream
Pineapple slices
Fresh peeled oranges
Fresh parsley sprigs

Rub pork roast with lemon, garlic clove and marjoram. Sprinkle with salt and pepper. Place seasoned pork loin in roaster and cook, uncovered, in 325° oven for 2½-3 hours or until meat thermometer registers 185° F. Remove roast from pan and keep warm. To make gravy, heat wine in pan juices. Stir in sour cream and season with salt and pepper. Serve gravy with pork loin. Garnish roast with pineapple slices, oranges and parsley sprigs. Serves 8.

Noodles with Poppy Seeds

16 ounces fettucini
½ cup butter, melted
2 teaspoons salt

¼ teaspoon white pepper
½ cup slivered almonds, toasted
4 teaspoons poppy seeds

Cook noodles according to package directions; drain and rinse under hot water. Place noodles in top of double boiler; stir in butter and remaining ingredients. Cover and keep hot over simmering water until serving time. Serves 8.

Brown Sugared Apricots

3 17-ounce cans apricots, drained
4 ounces Ritz crackers, crushed

1 cup brown sugar, firmly packed
½ cup butter, melted

Place drained apricots in bottom of 9x13x2-inch baking dish. Combine crushed crackers with brown sugar and crumble over fruit. Drizzle melted butter over fruit. Bake at 300° for 40 minutes. Serves 8.

Broccoli Stuffed Squash

8 medium yellow squash
1 chicken bouillon cube
10 ounces frozen chopped broccoli
½ cup cottage cheese
2 tablespoons grated Parmesan cheese
1 large egg, beaten

¼ teaspoon seasoned salt
¼ teaspoon onion salt
¼ teaspoon pepper
3 tablespoons dry bread crumbs
Paprika
No-stick vegetable cooking spray

Wash squash and trim ends. Drop into boiling water with bouillon cube. Cover and simmer 8-10 minutes or until tender but still firm. Drain and cool slightly. Cut squash in half lengthwise. Scoop out pulp, leaving firm shells; mash pulp. Cook broccoli according to package directions; drain well and add to squash pulp. Add cottage cheese and mix well. Stir in next 5 ingredients; spoon into squash shells. Sprinkle squash with bread crumbs and paprika. Place on baking sheet sprayed with vegetable cooking spray. Cover with foil and bake at 325° for 25 minutes. Uncover and bake 5 minutes. Serves 8.

Hearty Bran Biscuits

1 cup All-Bran cereal	2 tablespoons baking powder
1½ cups milk	1¼ teaspoons salt
2½ cups plain flour	¾ cup butter, softened

Combine cereal and milk; let stand 2 minutes. In mixing bowl, combine flour, baking powder and salt. Cut in butter until mixture resembles coarse meal. Add milk mixture and stir until ingredients are moistened. Turn dough onto lightly floured surface; knead 4-5 times. Roll dough to ½-inch thickness. Cut with a 2-inch biscuit cutter. Bake at 425° on ungreased baking sheet for 12-15 minutes or until lightly browned. Yield: 1 dozen.

Upside Down Lemon Meringue

½ cup sugar	½ cup sugar
⅛ teaspoon cream of tartar	¼ cup lemon juice
2 egg whites at room temperature	Grated rind of 1 lemon
	1 cup whipping cream
4 egg yolks	Lemon slices

Butter 9-inch glass pie plate. Sift together sugar and cream of tartar. Beat egg whites until stiff. Gradually add sifted mixture, beating until smooth and glossy. Spread mixture over bottom and sides of pie pan. Bake at 275 for 1 hour or until crisp to touch. Cool thoroughly before adding filling. In top of double boiler, beat egg yolks until thick and lemon colored. Add sugar and beat well. Stir in lemon juice and rind. Cook until thick, stirring constantly. Remove from heat and cool. Whip cream and fold into cooled filling. Pour filling into meringue shell. Cover with aluminum foil and refrigerate until ready to serve. Garnish with lemon slices. Serves 8.

Paris Mountain forms a dramatic backdrop to the northwest area of Greenville. According to legend the mountain was occupied by Cherokee Indians in early times and later became the property of Richard Pearis, for whom the mountain was named. Most historians agree that Pearis was the first white man to settle in the area.

In the mid-1800's, Altamont Hotel, a 23-room structure was built atop Paris Mountain and attracted visitors to the splendid view of the area. The hotel closed in the 1900's and the building was later used as Holmes Bible Institute.

Today, Paris Mountain is the site of many beautiful homes that lend themselves to gracious entertaining in the lush, mountain setting.

Up the Corporate Ladder Salute

Serves 8

Coquille St. Jâcques
Rice Verdae
Broiled Tomatoes
Asparagus Vinaigrette
Commercial Hard Rolls
Frozen Midnight Lady

Coquille St. Jâcques

2 tablespoons butter
2 tablespoons lemon juice
2 cups sliced mushrooms
3 pounds fresh scallops
2 tablespoons chives or grated onion
4 tablespoons dried parsley
1 cup sherry

½ cup water
4 tablespoons plain flour
1½ cups milk
Salt and pepper to taste
2 cups grated Jarlsberg cheese, divided
1 cup Italian bread crumbs

In large frying pan over medium heat, melt butter with lemon juice. Add mushrooms and cook for 5 minutes. Stir in scallops, chives, parsley, sherry and water; cover and cook for 5 minutes or until scallops are tender. Strain mixture, reserving liquid. Return liquid to pan and cook until liquid is reduced to 1 cup. Blend flour and milk; add to pan and cook, stirring constantly until thickened. Return scallop mixture to pan and season with salt and pepper. Add 1 cup of cheese. Pour mixture into 9x13x2-inch baking dish. Combine bread crumbs and remaining cheese and sprinkle over scallop mixture. Broil until brown. Serve over Rice Verdae. Swiss cheese may be used instead of Jarlsberg, if desired. Serves 8.

Rice Verdae

1½ cups raw rice
6 tablespoons butter, melted
Salt and pepper to taste

3 teaspoons dried dill weed
1 cup chopped fresh parsley
4 green onions, chopped

Cook rice in large pan of salted water until tender and fluffy. Do not overcook. Drain rice. If serving immediately, put rice in serving dish and top with butter. Season lightly with salt and pepper and toss with herbs and chopped onions. If rice is to be served later, rinse rice with cold water; drain well and set aside. When ready to serve, melt butter in large skillet, mix in seasonings, herbs and onions. Add rice, toss well, and cook until heated. Serve immediately. Serves 8.

Broiled Tomatoes

    4 tomatoes, halved   1 teaspoon oregano
       Salt and pepper to taste   ¼ cup butter, melted
    ½ cup grated Romano cheese

Place tomato halves in 9x13x2-inch baking dish and sprinkle with salt and
pepper. Broil for 5 minutes 4 inches from heat. Mix cheese with oregano
and sprinkle evenly over tops of tomato halves. Drizzle butter on each. Broil
until lightly browned. Serves 8.

Asparagus Vinaigrette

    40 fresh asparagus spears,   ½ teaspoon chopped onion
        steamed   1 tablespoon chopped pimento,
    ½ cup oil   drained
    ¼ cup wine vinegar   Lettuce leaves
    ½ teaspoon salt   4 bacon slices, cooked and
    ½ teaspoon dry mustard   crumbled

Place steamed asparagus in 9x13x2-inch baking dish. In a jar, combine
oil, vinegar, salt, mustard, onion and pimento. Shake well and pour
½ of dressing over asparagus. Cover and refrigerate. When ready to serve,
arrange asparagus spears on lettuce leaves. Shake remaining dressing and
pour over asparagus. Garnish with crumbled bacon. May use canned young
asparagus spears as substitute for fresh. Serves 8.

Frozen Midnight Lady

    2 3-ounce packages ladyfingers   22 ounces fudge ice cream
    1 quart vanilla ice cream   topping
    1 quart chocolate ice cream   12 ounces brickle bits
    1 quart coffee ice cream   Whipped cream, optional

Line sides and bottom of 10-inch springform pan with split ladyfingers,
standing rounded, uncut edges around inside of pan. Drop slightly softened
vanilla ice cream by scoopfuls into bottom of pan; smooth ice cream using
back of spoon or knife to form an even layer. Cover ice cream with ⅓ of
fudge topping. Sprinkle ⅓ of brickle bits over fudge topping. Continue
layering next 2 ice cream flavors and toppings as described above. Freeze
for at least 24 hours. Garnish with whipped cream before serving, if desired.
Serves 12-15.

Evening at the Symphony

Serves 8

Stuffed Artichoke Hearts
Perfect Standing Rib Roast
Dinner Jacket Potatoes
Fresh Green Beans Almondine
Bakery Croissants
Chocolate Torte Royale

Stuffed Artichoke Hearts

3 14-ounce cans artichoke hearts	1 tablespoon oregano
1 cup dry bread crumbs	1/2 teaspoon salt
1 tablespoon Parmesan cheese	Pepper to taste
1 tablespoon dried parsley	1/2 cup olive oil
2 cloves garlic, mashed	Butter
	Fresh parsley sprigs

Drain and rinse artichoke hearts. Place all ingredients except artichokes and butter in large bowl; mix well. Cut 1/4 from bottoms of artichoke hearts to form bases so they will stand up in pan. Separate artichoke leaves slightly and stuff with bread crumb mixture. Place on greased cookie sheet and top each with a small piece of butter. Bake at 425° for 15 minutes. Serve hot on small plates garnished with parsley sprigs. This is also a good stuffing for mushrooms. Can freeze before baking. Serves 8.

Perfect Standing Rib Roast

1 9-pound standing rib roast	Garlic powder
Soy sauce	Onion powder
Curry powder	

Preheat oven to 500°. With boning knife, carve ribs from roast and save. Rub roast generously with soy sauce and seasonings. Place roast on top of ribs in roasting pan. Bake for 30 minutes. Reduce heat to 300° and cook for 20 minutes per pound. Transfer roast from pan to carving platter and let stand 10 minutes before carving. Serves 8.

Dinner Jacket Potatoes

4 large baking potatoes	Salt and pepper to taste
1/2 cup butter	Parmesan cheese, grated
1 cup grated cheddar cheese	8 bacon slices, cooked and crumbled
1 cup sour cream	
1 cup milk	

continued

Scrub potatoes and bake at 400° for 1 hour or until done. Cut potatoes in half lengthwise and spoon pulp into large mixing bowl. Save shells. Beat hot potatoes with mixer until smooth. Add butter, cheddar cheese, sour cream, milk, salt and pepper; mix well. Spoon potato mixture into shells and place in large baking dish. Top with Parmesan cheese and bacon. Bake for 15 minutes at 350°. Serves 8.

Fresh Green Beans Almondine

1½ pounds fresh green beans
½ cup butter
1 teaspoon salt
1 teaspoon lemon pepper
¾ cup slivered almonds, toasted

Remove ends from beans and string if necessary. Wash beans. Steam 10-12 minutes or until crisp tender. Remove to serving dish. Melt butter and pour over beans. Add salt, lemon pepper and toasted almonds; toss well. Serve immediately. Serves 8.

Chocolate Torte Royale

3 egg whites
¼ teaspoon salt
½ teaspoon vinegar
½ cup sugar
¼ teaspoon cinnamon
6 ounces semi-sweet chocolate chips
2 egg yolks, beaten
¼ cup water
1 cup whipping cream
¼ cup sugar
¼ teaspoon cinnamon
1 cup whipping cream, whipped
½ cup finely chopped nuts

Cover a cookie sheet with heavy paper. Draw 8-inch circle in center. In bowl, beat egg whites, salt and vinegar until soft peaks form. Blend sugar and cinnamon. Gradually add to egg whites and beat until very stiff and all sugar is dissolved. Spread mixture within paper circle until bottom is ½ inch thick and edge stands 1½ inches high. Bake at 275° for 1 hour. Turn oven off and let dry in oven with door closed for 2 hours or overnight. Peel off paper and transfer to serving plate. Melt chocolate chips in double boiler. Cool. Spread two tablespoons chocolate inside cooled meringue. Add egg yolks and water to remaining chocolate and blend. Chill until mixture is thick. Combine 1 cup whipping cream, sugar and cinnamon; beat until stiff. Spread ½ of whipped cream over chocolate in shell. Fold remainder of whipped cream into chilled chocolate mixture and spread on top of meringue. Chill several hours or overnight. Just before serving, top with whipped cream and sprinkle with nuts. Serves 8.

Symphony concerts presented by the Greenville Symphony Association have been popular cultural events since 1949 when the Association was formed. Annually, the 80-piece orchestra presents a subscription series of six concerts as well as eleven concerts for children. Acclaimed as the best orchestra in South Carolina, the Greenville Symphony has earned a prominent position in the Southeast.

The Boss Comes to Dinner

Serves 6

Vichyssoise with Chives
Veal Scallops with Artichokes
Orange Rice Supreme
Crumb Topped Vegetable Trio
Fruit Medley
Almond Parfait

Vichyssoise with Chives

4 cups water
1 pound potatoes, diced
2 cups chopped onions
6 chicken bouillon cubes
¼ teaspoon white pepper
½ cup mayonnaise
Fresh chopped chives

Combine the first 5 ingredients in large saucepan; bring to boil over high
heat. Reduce to low heat and simmer 15 minutes or until potatoes are
tender. Cool. Place ½ of mixture in electric blender and blend until smooth.
Repeat with remainder of mixture and pour into large bowl. Whisk in
mayonnaise. Cover and chill overnight. Stir in chives 1 hour before serving.
Yield: 1 quart.

Veal Scallops with Artichokes

8 veal cutlets
Flour
Garlic powder
½ cup butter
4 tablespoons white wine
4 tablespoons lemon juice
6 tablespoons plain flour
2 cups water
2 14½-ounce cans chicken broth
8 green onions with tops,
chopped
1 cup sliced mushrooms
1 cup artichoke hearts

Pound veal cutlets until thin; roll in flour and pound cutlets again. Sprinkle
meat with garlic powder. Melt butter in skillet; add wine and lemon. Saute
veal in mixture until browned on both sides. Remove meat from pan.
Mix flour with water. Stir into pan drippings along with broth; cook until
thickened. Add onions, mushrooms and artichokes. Cook 5-10 minutes.
Add cutlets and simmer for 20 minutes or until tender. Serves 6.

Orange Rice Supreme

1 cup raw rice
½ cup butter, melted
1 10¾-ounce can chicken with
  rice soup
1¼ cups orange juice

1 8-ounce can sliced water
  chestnuts, drained
2 teaspoons grated orange rind
½ teaspoon seasoned salt

Combine all ingredients and pour into a 9x9-inch casserole dish. Bake at 300° for 1 hour. Serves 6.

Crumb Topped Vegetable Trio

1 cup butter
½ cup dry bread crumbs
4 hard-cooked eggs, chopped
2 tablespoons dried parsley
  Salt and pepper to taste

1 small bunch broccoli, cut into
  florets and steamed
1 small head cauliflower, cut
  into florets and steamed
¾ pound snow peas, steamed

Melt butter in saucepan until bubbly. Stir in bread crumbs. Mix well and cook until browned. Remove from heat. Stir in eggs, parsley, salt and pepper. To serve, arrange each variety of steamed vegetables in 9x13x2-inch baking dish. Sprinkle crumb mixture over top of vegetables. Serves 6.

Fruit Medley

1 16-ounce can pear halves
1 16-ounce can peach halves
1 16½-ounce can sweet
  cherries, pitted
1 15¼-ounce can pineapple
  chunks

1 17-ounce can apricot halves
1 15-ounce can spiced apples
½ cup butter
2 tablespoons plain flour
1 cup sherry

Drain fruit; place fruit in 9x13x2-inch baking dish. Melt butter; add flour and sherry and blend well. Pour over fruit. Refrigerate overnight. Bake at 350° for 25-30 minutes. Serves 8.

Almond Parfait

1¼ cups sugar
1¼ cups water
12 egg yolks
1½ teaspoons almond extract
3 tablespoons finely chopped almonds

1½ cups whipping cream, whipped
Whipped cream
Sliced almonds, toasted

Combine sugar and water in saucepan; bring to boil. Cook for 5 minutes, stirring constantly. Remove from heat and allow to cool. Pour syrup into top of double boiler. Beat egg yolks until lemony in color. Add 2 tablespoons of syrup to eggs. Beat again and add egg yolk mixture to syrup. Over simmering water, cook mixture, stirring constantly with wooden spoon, until it thickens and coats spoon. Remove from heat; stir until cool. Add almond flavoring and minced almonds to egg mixture. Fold in whipped cream. Pour mixture into parfait glasses and freeze. To serve, top with dollop of whipped cream and sprinkle with almonds. Serves 6.

Although Greenville is traditionally known as the "Textile Center of the World," the boss who comes to dinner now may be from a host of other industries as well. Greenville has become a diversified industrial and business center. Growth in the areas of electronics, chemical and tire manufacturing, pharmaceuticals and metal fabrications has brought progressive people and a bright future to Greenville and the upstate.

Fiesta Dinner

Serves 8

Baja Margarita
My Favorite Mexican Dip
Oven Tostada
South of the Border Lasagna
King Ranch Casserole
Mexican Rice
Caramel Custard Dessert

Baja Margarita

1 large lime	Crushed ice
1 cup tequila	Kosher salt
½ cup Triple Sec	

Squeeze juice from lime. Put lime juice in blender with tequila and Triple Sec. Fill container of blender ¾ full with crushed ice. Blend on high until frozen. Rub rims of cocktail glasses with lime and dip in salt. Fill glasses and serve. Extra margarita should be stored in freezer. Yield: 8 drinks.

My Favorite Mexican Dip

8 ounces cream cheese, softened	Dash of hot sauce
2 cups shredded mild cheddar cheese	1 4-ounce can chopped green chilies
1 tablespoon lemon juice	1 medium tomato, chopped
1 tablespoon chicken bouillon granules	1 tablespoon finely chopped onion

Combine the first 5 ingredients in mixing bowl; beat at medium speed until smooth. Drain chilies. Gently stir in chilies, tomatoes and onions. Put in serving bowl and chill. Serve with taco chips. Yield: 2 cups.

Oven Tostada

1 pound ground beef
1 medium onion, chopped
1 1½-ounce package taco
   seasoning mix
1 cup water
1 16-ounce can refried beans
1 8-ounce can crescent dinner
   rolls
¾ pound medium sharp cheese,
   grated

1 10-ounce bag corn chips,
   crushed
Shredded lettuce, optional
Diced tomato, optional
Diced avocado, optional
Sliced ripe olives, optional
Hot sauce, optional
Sour cream, optional
Grated sharp cheese, optional

Brown ground beef with onion and drain. Add taco seasoning, water and refried beans. Press crescent rolls into 7½x11¾-inch greased casserole dish forming a crust. Layer crushed corn chips over crust. Pour ground beef mixture on top. Cover with grated cheese. Bake at 350° for 25-30 minutes. Cut into squares and serve with condiments of your choice on top. Serves 8.

South of the Border Lasagna

1 pound ground beef
4 7-inch flour tortillas
½ cup oil
1 15-ounce can tomato sauce
2 teaspoons cumin
1 clove garlic, crushed
1 small onion, chopped

1 4-ounce can green chilies,
   chopped
6 ounces frozen avocado dip,
   thawed
4 ounces Monterey Jack cheese,
   grated

Brown meat in skillet; drain well. Fry tortillas in oil for about 5 seconds on each side until softened; drain well. Combine tomato sauce, cumin, garlic and onion in saucepan. Bring to a boil and simmer 10 minutes, uncovered. Remove ¼ cup of sauce from pan. Add beef and ½ green chilies to remaining sauce mixture. Place tortilla in greased 9-inch round pan. Top with ½ of meat mixture. Place second tortilla on meat. Top with avocado dip, ½ of cheese and remaining green chilies. Top with third tortilla and remaining meat mixture. Place last tortilla on meat and top with ¼ cup of reserved sauce. Bake uncovered at 350° for 40 minutes. Sprinkle with remaining cheese and bake for 5 minutes, or until cheese melts. Slice like a pie and serve immediately. Serves 8.

King Ranch Casserole

1 3-pound chicken
1 10-ounce can Rotel tomatoes
1 onion, diced
2 10¾ ounce cans cream of
   chicken soup
8 ounces sour cream
1 4-ounce can green chilies,
   chopped

1 package soft corn tortillas
½ pound Longhorn cheese,
   grated
½ pound Monterey Jack cheese,
   grated

Boil chicken; bone and cut into small pieces. Chop tomatoes. Add tomatoes
and onion to chicken. Mix soup, sour cream, and chilies in large bowl.
Tear tortillas into bite size pieces; set aside. Combine the cheeses. In
13x9x2-inch baking dish, layer as follows, using ½ of each item: chicken
mixture, tortillas, soup mixture and cheese. Repeat process with remaining
ingredients. Bake at 350° for 45 minutes. Serves 8.

Mexican Rice

2 tablespoons oil
1 cup raw rice
1 clove garlic, crushed
½ small onion, finely grated

1 teaspoon salt
½ teaspoon cumin
⅓ cup tomato sauce
2 cups water

Heat oil in saucepan; add rice and sauté until golden. Add garlic and onion;
sauté until onion is clear. Add salt, cumin, tomato sauce and water. Bring to
a boil and simmer for 25-30 minutes; do not stir. Cook until liquid is
absorbed. Stir before serving. Serves 8.

Caramel Custard Dessert

½ cup sugar
2½ tablespoons water
5 eggs, separated
1 13-ounce can evaporated milk

1 cup water
¾ cup sugar
1 tablespoon vanilla extract
⅛ teaspoon salt

Boil sugar and water until golden brown. Pour into 9-inch round pan; set
aside. Beat 3 egg whites and 5 egg yolks. Refrigerate remaining egg yolks
for other use. Add remaining ingredients. Stir well and pour onto golden
mixture in pan. Place pan in larger pan containing water. Bake at 325° for
1 hour. Cool and then chill several hours. Invert on serving dish. Serves 8.

The caramel custard dessert is a typical Mexican pudding and should be
thoroughly chilled before serving.
For a companion beverage choose traditional margaritas or cocktails with
a fruit juice base. Colorful straw mats, baskets, paper maché items and a
pinata centerpiece create a South of the Border atmosphere for the party.

Gourmet Anniversary Dinner

Serves 8

Low Country Crab Bisque
Baked Veal Marsala
Wonderful Asparagus
Rice Parmesan
Bakery Croissants
Rum Pie

Low Country Crab Bisque

1 cup Alaskan king crab meat,
  fresh or frozen, reserve liquid
  Sherry
1 10¾-ounce can cream of
  mushroom soup
1 10¾-ounce can cream of
  chicken soup
1 10¾-ounce can cream of
  celery soup
3 cups milk
  Dash cayenne pepper
2 teaspoons thyme
1 teaspoon celery seeds
4 tablespoons butter
  Paprika
  Fresh parsley sprigs

Soak crab meat in reserved liquid and enough sherry to cover. Mix soups with milk. Add crab meat and sherry to creamed mixture. Add seasonings and butter. Heat through. To serve, garnish with paprika and parsley. Serves 8.

Baked Veal Marsala

16 medium slices veal scalloppine
  Flour
4 tablespoons oil
  Paprika
4 tablespoons butter
¾ pound fresh mushrooms,
  sliced
3 tablespoons chopped dried
  parsley
3 tablespoons chopped dried
  chives
2 cups beef broth
  Salt and pepper to taste
¾ cup Marsala wine

Pound veal slices until very thin. Dust veal slices with flour. Heat oil in skillet. Sauté 3-4 slices of veal at a time over high heat until browned. Place veal slices in 9x13x2-inch baking dish and sprinkle each side lightly with paprika. Melt butter in saucepan and sauté mushrooms. Add parsley, chives, beef broth, salt, pepper and wine. Simmer 5 minutes. Pour mixture over veal slices and bake uncovered at 350° for 30 minutes. Serves 8.

Wonderful Asparagus

32 fresh asparagus spears
1½ cups sour cream
1 teaspoon garlic salt

1½ tablespoons horseradish
1½ tablespoons butter
¾ cup dry bread crumbs

Steam asparagus until crisp tender and place in 9x13x2-inch baking dish. Mix sour cream, garlic salt and horseradish; spread over asparagus. Melt butter and add bread crumbs. Sprinkle over asparagus. Broil until bread crumbs are browned. Serves 8.

Rice Parmesan

3 tablespoons butter
2 cups raw rice
½ cup chopped onion
¼ teaspoon saffron
2¾ cups beef broth

2 cups fresh grated Parmesan
cheese
½ cup butter, melted
Salt and pepper to taste

In heavy saucepan, melt 3 tablespoons butter. Sauté rice and onion until rice becomes opaque. Stir in saffron and beef broth. Bring rice mixture to a boil, then lower heat and simmer for 18 minutes; do not stir rice. Stir in 1 cup of Parmesan cheese, ½ cup butter, salt and pepper. Serve rice sprinkled with remaining Parmesan cheese. Serves 8.

Rum Pie

6 egg yolks
1 cup sugar
1 envelope unflavored gelatin
½ cup water
2 cups whipping cream

¼ cup rum
2 commercial graham cracker
crusts
Chocolate square

Beat egg yolks and sugar until very light. Dissolve gelatin in ½ cup water; bring to a boil. Add to egg and sugar mixture. Allow to set slightly. Whip cream and fold into mixture. Stir in rum. Pour into cracker crusts; cool in refrigerator. Shave chocolate on top to decorate. Yield: 2 pies.

After the Curtain Call

Serves 8

Cream of Almond Soup
Chicken Scallops with Lemon
Noodles Romanoff
Mushrooms with Tomatoes and Peas
Parmesan French Bread
Raspberries in Sherry Cream

Cream of Almond Soup

1 cup sliced almonds
½ cup butter
½ cup plain flour
2½ cups chicken broth
4 cups half-and-half
4 teaspoons instant minced onion

½ teaspoon salt
2 tablespoons dry sherry
Chopped fresh parsley
Sliced almonds for garnish

Crush almonds in food processor. Melt butter in saucepan over medium heat. Add almonds and sauté until lightly browned. Stir in flour. Gradually add broth and half-and-half and stir until smooth. Add onion and salt; cook until slightly thickened. When ready to serve, stir in sherry. Garnish each serving with chopped parsley and almond slices. Serves 8.

Chicken Scallops with Lemon

12 boneless chicken breast halves
Salt and pepper to taste
Flour
3 tablespoons butter
3 tablespoons olive oil

1 14½-ounce can chicken broth
12 thin slices of lemon
1½ tablespoons fresh lemon juice
3 tablespoons butter, softened

Skin chicken. Pound chicken breasts to ¼-inch thickness. Season with salt and pepper and dip in flour. In heavy skillet, melt 3 tablespoons butter in olive oil. Sauté chicken scallops for 2 minutes on each side; remove to platter. Pour off most of fat from skillet. Add ½ cup of chicken broth to remaining drippings and bring to boil. Return chicken scallops to pan and arrange lemon slices over top. Cover skillet and simmer 10-15 minutes until tender. To serve, transfer scallops to platter and surround with lemon slices. Add remaining chicken broth to pan juices and boil until glaze consistency. Add lemon juice and cook 1 minute. Remove from heat and swirl in remaining butter. Pour sauce over chicken and serve immediately. Veal may be substituted for chicken. Serves 8.

Noodles Romanoff

6 chicken bouillon cubes	1 small onion, chopped
6 cups boiling water	¾ teaspoon salt
12 ounces thin noodles	¼ teaspoon thyme
2 cups cottage cheese	½ teaspoon garlic salt
1½ cups sour cream	¾ cup dry bread crumbs

Preheat oven to 350°. Dissolve chicken bouillon cubes in boiling water. Add noodles and cook for 5 minutes, until tender. Stir all remaining ingredients except bread crumbs into drained noodles. Mix well. Pour into 9x13x2-inch baking dish and top with bread crumbs. Bake uncovered at 350° for 25 minutes. Serves 8.

Mushrooms with Tomatoes and Peas

2 medium onions, sliced	4 teaspoons lemon juice
1 teaspoon ground turmeric	2 teaspoons salt
½ teaspoon ground ginger	4 medium tomatoes, cut into
2 tablespoons oil	wedges
1 pound whole fresh mushrooms	
2 10-ounce packages frozen green peas, thawed and drained	

Cook and stir onion, turmeric and ginger in oil in 10-inch skillet over medium heat until onion is tender, about 3 minutes. Stir in mushrooms, peas, lemon juice and salt. Cook uncovered, stirring occasionally, until peas are tender, about 8 minutes. Stir in tomatoes; heat just until hot. Serves 8.

Parmesan French Bread

1 loaf French bread	½ cup grated Parmesan cheese
1 cup mayonnaise	1 teaspoon grated onion

Slice French bread lengthwise. Combine remaining ingredients. Spread mixture on cut sides of bread. Place both halves on cookie sheet. Bake at 350° for 20 minutes or until bubbly and lightly browned. Serves 8.

Raspberries in Sherry Cream

1 quart fresh red raspberries	2 tablespoons dry sherry
1 cup whipping cream	½ teaspoon almond extract
2 large eggs	Pinch of salt
2 tablespoons sugar	

Wash berries and chill until ready to serve. Heat cream in top of double boiler. Separate eggs and beat yolks with sugar until smooth. Pour small amount of hot cream into yolks, beating constantly. Pour egg mixture into remaining hot cream, beating constantly to avoid lumping. Continue to cook until mixture has thickened. Add sherry, almond extract, and salt to cream sauce. Beat egg whites until stiff and fold into sauce. When ready to serve, spoon chilled berries into individual serving dishes and top with cream sauce. Canned blackberries may be substituted. Cream sauce can be prepared ahead and served cold. Serves 8.

Curtain calls seem almost routine in Greenville as each of its three community theatres offers quality entertainment ranging from dramas and musicals to classics and contemporary hits.

The Greenville Little Theatre's beginnings can be traced back to 1926 and the production of three one-act plays. Over the years, it has developed into a prestigious cultural organization with five full productions annually. It is recognized as one of the top ten community theatres in the country.

Two other community theaters have in recent years broadened the scope of available theater. The Warehouse Theater was founded in 1974 as an alternative theater, offering a wide range of productions. Greenville's youngest theater is Center Stage whose troupe offers unique productions.

Elegant Old South Dinner

Serves 8

Shrimp Pâté
Spinach-Mushroom Stuffed Pork Chops
Carrots Grand Marnier
Gourmet Potatoes
Blue Cheese and Apple Vinaigrette
Parsley Biscuits
Bavarian Cream Goodness

Shrimp Pâté

1½ teaspoons unflavored gelatin
½ cup water
8 ounces cream cheese,
   softened
1 cup mayonnaise
2 cups cooked shrimp
½ cup chopped celery
2 teaspoons grated onion

Dissolve gelatin in water. Mix in remaining ingredients and chill overnight. Serve with assorted crackers. Yield: 4 cups.

Spinach-Mushroom Stuffed Pork Chops

10 ounces frozen chopped
   spinach
½ cup chopped onion
¾ cup chopped mushrooms
½ teaspoon salt
⅛ teaspoon pepper
¼ teaspoon nutmeg
8 pork chops, 1-inch thick
   Salt and pepper
⅓ cup plain flour
3 tablespoons butter
1½ cups white wine

Thaw and drain spinach. To prepare stuffing, combine spinach, onion, mushrooms, salt, pepper and nutmeg. Cut a pocket into side of each chop and stuff with spinach mixture. Secure openings with toothpicks. Salt and pepper chops. Roll each chop in flour and brown in butter in large skillet. When chops are browned, transfer to 9x13x2-inch baking dish. Add wine to skillet and stir until smooth. Pour wine sauce over chops, cover and bake at 350° for 1 hour. Remove cover and bake additional 20 minutes or until tender. Remove chops to serving platter. Return juices to skillet and thicken with flour to make gravy. Serve gravy with pork chops. Serves 8.

Carrots Grand Marnier

2 pounds carrots
6 tablespoons butter
1¼ cups sugar, divided

1 12-ounce jar orange
  marmalade
½ cup Grand Marnier

Peel and slice carrots into thin rounds. Steam or boil carrots until just tender. In large skillet, melt butter over medium heat. Add 1 cup sugar and marmalade and simmer until sugar is melted, 5-10 minutes. Add cooked carrots, remaining ¼ cup sugar and Grand Marnier. Simmer uncovered until carrots are shiny and candied, about 30 minutes. Carrots may be prepared a day ahead and reheated. Serves 8.

Gourmet Potatoes

9 medium potatoes
¾ cup butter
2 medium onions, chopped
1 pound mushrooms, sliced
1 cup hot milk

Salt and pepper to taste
1 cup sour cream
¼ cup butter, melted
Paprika

Peel and boil potatoes. Melt butter in skillet; sauté onions and mushrooms for 2 minutes. Remove onions and mushrooms, reserving butter. Drain and whip potatoes. Add hot milk, reserved butter, salt and pepper. In greased 9x13x2-inch baking dish, layer ⅓ potatoes, top with ½ sautéed vegetables and ½ cup sour cream. Repeat potato, vegetable and sour cream layers. Top with remaining potatoes. Drizzle with butter and sprinkle with paprika. Bake at 350° for 20-30 minutes. Serves 8.

Blue Cheese and Apple Vinaigrette

1 cup oil
½ cup sugar
½ cup cider vinegar
½ teaspoon salt
½ teaspoon dry mustard
1 teaspoon paprika

Mixed salad greens
1 red onion, sliced into rings
2 large Granny Smith apples,
  chopped
4 ounces blue cheese, crumbled

To prepare dressing, combine first 6 ingredients in a jar and shake well. Just before serving, arrange salad greens on individual plates. Layer onion rings, chopped apples and blue cheese over greens. Top with dressing. Serves 8.

Parsley Biscuits

2 cups unsifted plain flour
3 teaspoons baking powder
1 teaspoon salt

¼ cup chopped dried parsley
⅓ cup shortening
¾ cup milk

Into bowl sift flour, baking powder and salt; add parsley. Cut in shortening with pastry blender until mixture resembles coarse crumbs. Make well in flour; pour in milk. Stir until dough forms a soft ball. Turn dough onto lightly floured surface; coat dough with flour and knead 8-10 times. Roll dough to ½-inch thickness. Cut dough with 1½-inch floured biscuit cutter; place biscuits on ungreased baking sheet. Bake at 425° for 12-15 minutes, until lightly browned. Yield: 24 biscuits.

Bavarian Cream Goodness

1 angel food cake mix
1 envelope unflavored gelatin
¼ cup cold water
1 tablespoon plain flour
1 cup sugar
4 eggs, separated

Pinch of salt
2 cups milk
1 teaspoon almond extract
1 cup whipping cream
2 tablespoons powdered sugar
13½ ounces flaked coconut

Prepare angel food cake according to package directions and bake in tube pan. Dissolve gelatin in water. To prepare custard; mix flour and sugar in saucepan. Add egg yolks and salt; mix well. Gradually add milk. Cook over medium heat, stirring until thickened. Remove from heat and stir in dissolved gelatin. Let mixture cool. Beat egg whites until stiff and fold into custard. Add almond extract and set aside. To assemble dessert, slice cake horizontally into three layers. Place one layer in 10-inch springform pan. Using one of remaining layers, cut a piece of cake to fill the center hole of first layer. Spread ½ custard over cake layer. Place remaining cake layer on custard, fill center hole as described above. Top with remaining custard. Cover with foil and refrigerate overnight. Whip cream with powdered sugar and spread on top. Sprinkle with coconut. Remove collar from springform pan and place dessert on footed cake stand to serve. Serves 10.

Greek Gala

Serves 8

Cheese Squares
Dolmades with Avgolemono Sauce
Greek Salad
Almond Pie

Cheese Squares

1 cup milk
6 tablespoons butter, melted
4 tablespoons cream of wheat
½ pound feta cheese, crumbled
8 ounces cream cheese

8 ounces cottage cheese
¼ cup grated Romano cheese
4 large eggs
10 sheets phyllo pastry

Preheat oven to 350°. In sauce pan, heat milk slowly with ½ of butter. Add cream of wheat and continue stirring until slightly thickened. In separate bowl, mix cheeses with eggs. Add cream of wheat mixture and blend thoroughly with electric mixer at medium speed. With some of remaining butter, generously butter 5 sheets of phyllo pastry and arrange in bottom of 7½x11¾-inch baking dish. Top with cheese mixture. Butter remaining 5 sheets of pastry and cover cheese mixture. Bake 30-40 minutes until golden brown. Yield: 24 squares.

Dolmades with Avgolemono Sauce

1 medium head cabbage
1 pound lean ground beef,
  uncooked
1 medium onion, finely chopped
1 cup raw rice
2 teaspoons dried parsley
¼ cup lemon juice

1 teaspoon salt
¼ teaspoon pepper
4 tablespoons butter
2 cups beef broth
3 eggs, separated
  Juice of 2 lemons

Discard outer course leaves of cabbage; cut out tough stalk. Parboil cabbage. Set aside to cool. Combine ground beef with onion, rice, parsley, lemon juice, salt and pepper; mix well. To prepare Dolmades, place 1 tablespoon of meat filling on a cabbage leaf and roll, folding in ends of leaf. In Dutch oven, arrange Dolmades in layers; cover with plate to keep them in order. Add butter and beef broth. Cover and cook over low heat for 45-60 minutes. To prepare Avgolemono sauce, beat egg whites until fluffy. Gradually add yolks to whites, beating well. Slowly add hot, not boiling, broth from cooked Dolmades until all broth is used. Add lemon juice. Pour over Dolmades and serve. Yield: 14-16 Dolmades.

Greek Salad

1 head iceberg lettuce
1 small onion, chopped
2 medium tomatoes, chopped
4 ounces feta cheese, crumbled
1 cup pitted ripe olives
⅓ cup oil

⅓ cup olive oil
⅓ cup red wine vinegar
1 tablespoon oregano
2 teaspoons salt
1 teaspoon pepper
  Dash of garlic powder

Wash and tear lettuce and combine with onion, tomatoes, feta cheese and olives. To prepare dressing, combine remaining ingredients; mix well. Just before serving, toss salad ingredients with dressing. Serves 8.

Almond Pie

6 egg whites
1½ cups sugar
2 cups finely chopped pecans
1⅓ cups graham cracker crumbs
2 teaspoons baking powder

2 teaspoons almond extract
2 cups whipping cream
6 tablespoons powdered sugar
1 teaspoon almond extract

Grease two 9-inch pie pans. Preheat oven to 300°. Gradually add sugar while beating egg whites until stiff. Stir in pecans, cracker crumbs, baking powder and 2 teaspoons almond extract. Pour into pie pans. Bake for 30 minutes. Let cool. Pies will fall. In a bowl, combine whipping cream, powdered sugar and 1 teaspoon almond extract and beat until stiff. Ice pies with whipped cream. Yield: 2 pies.

Good food and the Greek community in Greenville go hand in hand. Many Greek families own restaurants in the area and the Greek Ladies Philoptochos sponsors several luncheons and bake sales annually featuring their delicious traditional dishes. The proceeds from these sales go to over 100 civic organizations that are supported by the women of the St. George Greek Orthodox Church.

House Guests' Favorite Dinner

Serves 8

New England Clam Chowder
Shrimp and Scallops Sevilla
Lemon Rice
Layered Salad Supreme
Bakery Potato Rolls
Lou Parks' German Chocolate Pie

New England Clam Chowder

12 bacon slices
½ cup minced onion
2 10½-ounce cans cream of
   potato soup
2 cups half-and-half

2 10-ounce cans of
   minced clams
2 tablespoons fresh lemon juice
¼ teaspoon black pepper

Fry bacon and break into large pieces. Do not drain clams. In a medium saucepan, add bacon pieces to remaining ingredients and cook over medium heat until hot, stirring constantly. Serves 8.

Shrimp and Scallops Sevilla

1 pound medium shrimp
1 pound scallops
1 clove garlic, peeled
½ cup olive oil

½ cup dry sherry
½ cup fresh chopped parsley
   Salt and pepper to taste

Peel and devein shrimp. Wash seafood in cold water and dry on clean towel. In Dutch oven, brown garlic in olive oil over medium low heat. Remove garlic and discard. Slide seafood into pan to avoid splattering. Saute 3-4 minutes. Add sherry and parsley. Cook 2-3 minutes. Add salt and pepper to taste. Can be prepared to this point and allowed to sit until ready to serve. Reheat before serving. Serve over Lemon Rice. Serves 8.

Lemon Rice

4 tablespoons butter
1¾ cups raw rice
½ cup dry vermouth
3¼ cups chicken broth
1¼ teaspoon salt

Dash white pepper
Rind of 1 lemon, coarsely
grated
2 tablespoons dried parsley

Melt butter in a skillet over medium heat. Add rice and stir until all grains are coated with butter. Add vermouth, broth, salt and pepper. Bring to boil. Pour into 2-quart round baking dish. Cover and bake at 350° for 35-45 minutes or until fluffy. To serve, toss with lemon rind and parsley. Serves 8.

Layered Salad Supreme

1 10-ounce package fresh
  spinach
Salt and pepper to taste
½ tablespoon sugar
6 bacon slices, cooked and
  crumbled
3 hard-cooked eggs, sliced
  Iceberg lettuce, washed and
  torn
  Salt and pepper
1 teaspoon sugar
2 cups sliced fresh mushrooms
½ cup chopped pecans
1 10-ounce package frozen
  green peas
  Salt and pepper to taste
1 teaspoon sugar
½ cup chopped pecans
2 cups mayonnaise
1 cup grated Swiss cheese
  Paprika
  Cherry tomatoes, halved or
  quartered

Wash and stem spinach; wash and slice mushrooms; thaw green peas and drain. Assemble in a 9x13x2-inch casserole by layering all ingredients except tomatoes in order listed above. Refrigerate 24 hours. May be made up to 48 hours in advance. When ready to serve, garnish salad with cherry tomato halves or quarters. Serves 8.

Lou Parks' German Chocolate Pie

2 egg whites
⅛ teaspoon salt
⅛ teaspoon cream of tartar
½ cup sugar
½ teaspoon vanilla extract
½ cup finely chopped walnuts or
  pecans
3 tablespoons water
1 4-ounce bar milk chocolate
1 cup whipping cream

To make crust, beat egg whites, salt and cream of tartar until foamy. Add sugar, 2 tablespoons at a time, beating well until very stiff peaks form. Fold in vanilla and nuts. Spoon meringue mixture into a lightly-greased 8-inch deep dish pie pan, forming a shell with sides that extend ½ inch above edge of pie pan. Bake at 300° for 50-60 minutes. Remove from oven and cool.
To prepare filling, place water in small saucepan; break chocolate bar into water and heat slowly until melted. Cool until thickened. Whip cream and fold into chocolate. Spoon chocolate filling into meringue crust and chill at least 2 hours before serving. Serves 8.

When hosting out-of-town guests, plan this menu for their first night in your home. While you and the house are still "fresh," it is the perfect time to invite other friends to meet your guests and to enjoy this easy-to-prepare meal.

Baby Boomer Board Game Party

Serves 8

Hot Mushroom Meringues
Chicken Parmesan
Herbed Fettucini
Italian House Salad
Coffee Spumoni

Hot Mushroom Meringues

$\frac{1}{2}$ pound fresh mushrooms
2 tablespoons butter
$\frac{1}{4}$ teaspoon salt
$\frac{1}{8}$ teaspoon pepper
$\frac{1}{4}$ teaspoon garlic powder

2 eggs, separated
2 tablespoons heavy cream
10 slices white bread
Parmesan cheese, grated

Clean and finely chop mushrooms and sauté in butter. Season with salt, pepper and garlic powder. Combine slightly beaten egg yolks with cream and add to mushrooms. Continue to cook over low heat until thickened, about 5 minutes. Cut bread slices with biscuit cutter into 2-inch rounds. Spread with mushroom mixture. Sprinkle with Parmesan cheese. Beat egg whites until stiff. With spatula ice entire surface of bread. Bake at 400° on lightly greased baking sheet until meringues are delicately browned, about 10-15 minutes. Serve immediately. Yield: 10 meringues.

Chicken Parmesan

1 cup plain flour
1 teaspoon garlic salt
Dash pepper
8 boneless chicken breast halves
1 cup dried bread crumbs
2 teaspoons oregano
$\frac{1}{2}$ cup grated Parmesan cheese

2 eggs, beaten
4 tablespoons olive oil
8 thin slices mozzarella cheese
42 ounces commercial spaghetti
  sauce
1 cup water
$\frac{1}{2}$ cup grated Parmesan cheese

Combine flour, garlic salt and pepper; coat chicken. Mix bread crumbs, $\frac{1}{2}$ cup Parmesan cheese and oregano. Dip chicken breasts in egg, then in crumb mixture. Brown chicken slowly in hot oil. Remove chicken breasts to baking dish. Place slice of mozzarella cheese on each chicken breast. Mix spaghetti sauce with water and pour over chicken. Sprinkle with $\frac{1}{2}$ cup Parmesan cheese. Cover and bake at 350° for 30 minutes. Remove chicken to serving platter; spoon extra sauce over chicken. Serves 8.

Herbed Fettucini

1 pound fettucini
4 quarts water
¾ cup butter
¾ cup light cream
1½ cups grated Parmesan cheese
2 teaspoons dried parsley

1 teaspoon dried thyme
1 teaspoon dried basil
1 teaspoon snipped chives
¼ teaspoon salt
Dash pepper

Cook noodles in boiling water for 8-10 minutes, or until tender. Place butter and cream in small saucepan over low heat until butter melts. Stir in cheese, herbs and seasonings. Keep sauce warm over low heat. Drain noodles and return to pot. Pour sauce over noodles, stirring gently until well coated. Serves 8.

Italian House Salad

1 large head lettuce
1 small head cauliflower
1 large purple onion
1 cup pitted black olives
¼ cup vinegar

¾ cup oil
1 teaspoon salt
1 teaspoon sugar
¼ teaspoon dry mustard
¼ teaspoon black pepper

Break lettuce into large salad bowl. Cut cauliflower into bitesize florets and add to lettuce. Slice onion and olives into thin rings and add to bowl. To prepare dressing, put remaining ingredients in jar and shake well; chill. Before serving toss salad with dressing. Serves 8.

Coffee Spumoni

½ gallon coffee ice cream
½ cup coarsely chopped pecans
1 tablespoon butter
12 almond macaroons, crumbled

⅛ cup bourbon
1 cup whipping cream, whipped
Pecan halves

Let ice cream soften. Toast chopped pecans lightly in butter. Butter a 9-inch square pan. Sprinkle ⅔ of macaroon crumbs in pan, reserving ⅓ of crumbs for topping. Mix bourbon in ice cream. Spread ½ of ice cream over crumbs. Sprinkle with toasted pecans. Spread remaining ice cream over pecans and top with remaining crumbs. Freeze. Cut into 8 squares to serve. Garnish with whipped cream and pecan halves. Serves 8.

Baby Boomers grew up with board game classics like Scrabble and Monopoly. For after dinner fun, bring out the gang's favorite games, whether old or new, and retest skills rewarding good plays with boxes of Cracker Jacks to munch on!

Celebrate His Birthday

Serves 12

Bacon Mushroom Caps
Crab Pâté
Crown Roast of Pork with Fruit Dressing
Cumberland Sauce
Frosted Cauliflower Supreme
Marinated Bean Bundles
Bakery Yeast Rolls
Devil's Food Spectacular

Bacon Mushroom Caps

8 ounces cream cheese,
  softened
1 medium onion, grated

12 bacon slices, fried and
  crumbled
2 pounds large mushrooms

Blend together cream cheese, onion and bacon. Remove stems from mushrooms; discard stems. Fill caps with cream cheese mixture. Microwave for 3 minutes on high. Serve immediately. Yield: 12 servings.

Crab Pâté

1 10¾-ounce can cream of
  mushroom soup
1 envelope unflavored gelatin
3 tablespoons cold water
¾ cup mayonnaise
8 ounces cream cheese,
  softened

1 cup crab meat, drained and
  flaked
1 small onion, grated
1 cup finely chopped celery
Fresh parsley

Heat soup in a medium saucepan over low heat; remove from heat. Dissolve gelatin in cold water; add to soup. Add next 5 ingredients and mix well. Spoon into a greased 4-cup mold. Chill until firm. Unmold and garnish with fresh parsley. Serve with crackers. Yield: 4 cups.

Crown Roast of Pork with Fruit Dressing

1 8-pound crown roast of pork
Lemon juice
Salt and pepper
½ cup Dijon-style mustard
2 tablespoons soy sauce
2 garlic cloves, minced
1 teaspoon sage
¼ teaspoon marjoram
2 tablespoons butter
2 medium onions, chopped
1 cup chopped celery
1 cup dried bread crumbs
2 cups cooked rice
½ teaspoon marjoram

½ teaspoon thyme
Dash of sage
Salt and pepper to taste
2 7-ounce cans pineapple
tidbits, drained
1 cup orange sections, cut into
pieces
½ cup golden raisins
¼ cup blanched slivered almonds
½ cup dry white wine
Paper frills
Lettuce leaves
Cherry tomatoes

Preheat oven to 325°. Remove all fat from roast. Moisten paper towel with lemon juice and rub over roast. Place roast on rack in roasting pan; sprinkle with salt and pepper. Cover exposed ends of bones with foil to prevent burning; crumble additional foil and place in center of roast to retain shape. Roast for 1 hour. Combine mustard, soy sauce, garlic, sage and marjoram. Baste roast with sauce. Continue cooking for another hour, basting roast after 30 minutes with pan juices. Remove foil from center of roast and paint the inside with pan juices. To prepare dressing, melt butter in skillet over low heat. Add onions and celery; sauté until tender. Stir in bread crumbs, rice, marjoram, thyme, sage, salt and pepper. Add remaining ingredients and stir to combine. Pack dressing into center of roast. Cover dressing with foil and continue cooking for 1½ hours or until meat thermometer registers 170°. Remove roast from oven; remove foil. Cover bone tips with paper frills. Garnish base of roast with fancy lettuce leaves and cherry tomatoes. Serve roast with Cumberland Sauce on the side. Serves 12.

Cumberland Sauce

1½ cups red currant jelly
½ cup ruby port wine
Juice of 2 oranges
2 tablespoons fresh lemon juice

2 tablespoons prepared mustard
2 teaspoons paprika
1 teaspoon ginger
Grated peel of 2 oranges

Melt jelly in 1-quart saucepan over low heat. Add wine, orange juice, lemon juice, mustard, paprika and ginger. Simmer a few minutes, stirring occasionally. Add orange peel and cook for one minute. Can be prepared ahead of time and refrigerated until needed; heat through before serving. Yield: 2 cups.

Frosted Cauliflower Supreme

2 medium heads cauliflower
¾ cup mayonnaise
½ cup grated Parmesan cheese

2¼ teaspoons dried parsley flakes
3 egg whites, stiffly beaten

Steam or simmer the cauliflower head for about 15 minutes or until it is crisp tender. Blend together the mayonnaise, Parmesan cheese and parsley flakes. Add the stiffly beaten egg whites to the mayonnaise mixture. Coat cauliflower with sauce. Bake at 350° for 15 minutes or until the frosting begins to brown. Remove whole cauliflower to serving dish. Before serving, cut into pie-shaped wedges and garnish with fresh parsley. Serves 12.

Marinated Bean Bundles

2 pounds fresh green beans
1 cup commercial Italian
   dressing

3 small red sweet peppers

Wash beans and remove strings. Cook whole beans, covered, in a small amount of boiling water for 10 minutes or until crisp tender. Drain beans and cool. Cut red peppers into 12 rings. Divide beans into 12 bundles and carefully place each bundle through a pepper ring. Arrange bundles in dish and pour dressing over beans. Cover and refrigerate at least 2 hours; basting frequently. To serve, arrange on silver serving platter. Serves 12.

Devil's Food Spectacular

2¼ cups cake flour
2 teaspoons baking soda
½ teaspoon salt
½ cup butter
2½ cups brown sugar, firmly
   packed
3 eggs
4 ounces unsweetened chocolate

½ cup buttermilk
2 teaspoons vanilla extract
1 cup boiling water
3 cups whipping cream
½ cup sugar
4 tablespoons cocoa
1 teaspoon vanilla extract

Grease and flour three 8-inch cake pans. Sift cake flour, measure carefully and sift again with soda and salt. In mixing bowl, cream butter until soft. Gradually add sugar and beat until fluffy. Add unbeaten eggs one at a time; beating well after each addition. Melt chocolate; add to cream mixture, blending thoroughly. Sift ⅓ of flour mixture into batter; mix well. Add ¼ cup buttermilk; stir slightly. Alternate flour and buttermilk as described above, ending with flour. Stir in vanilla and boiling water. Batter will be thin. Pour batter into cake pans. Bake at 375° for 25-30 minutes. Cool cake layers 10 minutes; remove from pans and cool completely. Prepare frosting by combining cream, sugar, cocoa and vanilla; refrigerate for 2 hours. Remove mixture from refrigerator and beat frosting until stiff peaks form. Spread frosting between layers. Frost top and sides of cake. Store cake in refrigerator. To serve, garnish with chocolate curls. Serves 12.

Remembering Whitehall

Serves 8

Lemon Soup
Ginger Pear Chicken
French Quarter Green Beans
Easy Mushroom Rice
Mimi's Rolls
Strawberries on a Cloud

Lemon Soup

2 quarts chicken broth
5 celery stalks, chopped
1 carrot, chopped
1 large onion, chopped

Salt and pepper to taste
3 egg yolks
Juice of 1 lemon
Lemon slices

Simmer broth, celery, carrot and onion for 1 hour. Add salt and pepper. In double boiler beat egg yolks and slowly add lemon juice. Continue beating. Strain broth and add to egg mixture while both are still warm, stirring quickly. Serve with a slice of lemon on top. Good hot or cold. Yield: 16 cups.

Ginger Pear Chicken

8 boneless chicken breast halves
¼ cup butter
    Salt to taste
2 16-ounce cans pear halves
2 cups ginger ale
½ cup brown sugar, firmly
    packed

4 tablespoons vinegar
5 tablespoons soy sauce
1 tablespoon powdered ginger
4 tablespoons cornstarch
½ cup water
½ cup toasted pecan halves

Remove skins from chicken breasts. Lightly brown in butter over medium heat. Salt to taste. Drain pears and reserve liquid. Mix ginger ale, brown sugar, vinegar, soy sauce and ginger. Add to chicken along with reserved pear juice. Simmer for 1 hour adding additional ginger ale if needed. Remove chicken to warm plate. Make a paste out of cornstarch and water. Add to slightly cooled liquid in frying pan. When sauce thickens, return chicken to pan and add pears and toasted pecans. Cook slowly for 10-12 minutes. Serves 8.

French Quarter Green Beans

3 9-ounce packages frozen
   French-style green beans
3 tablespoons butter
1 10¾ ounce can cream of
   mushroom soup
3 ounces cream cheese,
   softened
1 teaspoon dried onion flakes
8 ounces water chestnuts, sliced
¼ teaspoon garlic salt
¼ teaspoon pepper
1½ cups shredded cheddar cheese
2½ ounces slivered almonds
   Paprika

Cook green beans according to package directions; drain. Melt butter in Dutch oven. Add soup and cream cheese. Cook over low heat, stirring constantly, until cream cheese is melted and mixture is smooth. Remove from heat. Stir in green beans, onion flakes, water chestnuts, garlic salt, pepper and cheddar cheese. Spoon mixture into lightly greased 1¾-quart casserole. Top with almonds, if desired. Sprinkle with paprika. Bake uncovered at 375° for 45 minutes. Yield: 8 servings.

Easy Mushroom Rice

6 tablespoons butter
8 ounces fresh mushrooms,
   sliced
1 teaspoon salt
1 tablespoon dried parsley flakes
4 cups cooked rice

In large skillet sauté mushrooms in butter. Add salt. To serve, toss mushrooms and parsley flakes with cooked rice. Serves 8.

Mimi's Rolls

1½ packages active dry yeast
¼ cup warm water
½ cup sugar, reserve 1
   tablespoon
1 teaspoon salt
½ cup butter, melted
1 cup milk
2 eggs, beaten
4½ cups plain flour

Sprinkle yeast over warm water and add 1 tablespoon of sugar; mix together and let stand in warm place for 10 minutes. Combine remaining sugar and salt in bowl. Melt butter; add milk and scald. Combine butter/milk mixture with sugar and salt mixture; allow to cool slightly. Add yeast mixture. Beat in eggs and flour and place in greased bowl. Cover and let rise in warm place until doubled in bulk, 1-2 hours. Turn onto floured board and divide into 4 parts. Roll each part into circle ⅛-inch thick. Cut into 12 pie-shaped pieces. Dip the large end into melted butter and roll up. Place on greased baking sheet and let rise until doubled in bulk, 1-2 hours. Bake at 375° for 10-15 minutes. Yield: 48 rolls.

Strawberries on a Cloud

4 egg whites
1/4 teaspoon salt
1/4 teaspoon cream of tartar
1 cup sugar
4 teaspoons cornstarch

2 teaspoons vinegar
2 teaspoons vanilla extract
1 cup whipping cream, whipped
3 cups strawberries, sliced
Grand Marnier

Beat egg whites, salt and cream of tartar until stiff peaks form. Gradually add sugar, beating until mixture is glossy. Beat in cornstarch, then vinegar and vanilla. Fill buttered and floured 9-inch springform pan with mixture, mounding around edges to form a shell. Bake at 275° for 1½ hours or until dry. Cool and unmold onto plate. Sprinkle strawberries with Grand Marnier. Before serving, fill meringue shell with whipped cream. To serve, cut meringue into wedges. Top individual servings with strawberries. Serve immediately. Serves 8.

Antebellum Whitehall, constructed in 1813, is the oldest house still standing in Greenville and remains at its original location at 310 West Earle Street. Whitehall was built by Henry Middleton, owner of the well-known Middleton Gardens in Charleston. A United States senator, governor of South Carolina, and minister to Russia, he was the son of Arthur Middleton, a signer of the Declaration of Independence. The structure, a rare example of the Charleston-style summer house, was built as a refuge from the summer heat of the South Carolina coast. The Earle family bought Whitehall from Middleton and descendants of the Earles have lived in the house for five generations. Whitehall is located in the Earle Street Historic District along with many other homes of historical interest.

Couples for Bridge

Serves 8

Chicken Kabobs
Confetti Rice
Spinach Salad
Italian Bread with Garlic Butter
Mocha Almond Parfaits

Chicken Kabobs

1 12-ounce can pineapple chunks	1 teaspoon garlic salt
½ cup soy sauce	¼ teaspoon pepper
¼ cup oil	10 boneless chicken breast halves
1 teaspoon dry mustard	12 bacon slices
1 tablespoon brown sugar	3 zucchini, cut into 1-inch slices
2 teaspoons ground ginger	16 large mushrooms
	16 small onions, parboiled

Drain pineapple chunks, reserving ½ cup juice. Refrigerate chunks until ready to skewer. In a small saucepan, combine soy sauce, pineapple juice, oil, mustard, brown sugar, ginger, garlic salt, and pepper; simmer for 5 minutes. Cool. Cut chicken breasts into 1¼-inch pieces. Pour marinade over chicken pieces and marinate in refrigerator for at least 6 hours, preferably overnight. To assemble, wrap each chicken piece with ⅓ slice bacon. Thread chicken on skewers, alternating remaining ingredients by color. Grill over slow to medium hot coals for 15-20 minutes, basting frequently with marinade. Serves 8.

Confetti Rice

½ cup butter	3 10¾-ounce cans chicken broth
1 cup finely chopped celery	1½ cups raw rice
1 cup finely chopped onion	¼ cup dried parsley
1 bell pepper, finely chopped	

Preheat oven to 350°. Melt butter in skillet; sauté next 3 ingredients for 5 minutes. Do not brown. Pour broth into 2-quart baking dish; add rice, stirring for 3 minutes. Add sautéed vegetables. Cover dish and bake for 45 minutes. Immediately before serving, toss rice with parsley. Serves 8.

Spinach Salad

2 pounds spinach
½ cup coarsely chopped walnuts
8 bacon slices, fried and crumbled
4 hard-cooked eggs, sliced
½ cup fresh mushrooms, sliced
2 tomatoes, cut in wedges, optional

1 can bean sprouts, optional
1 cup oil
¾ cup ketchup
1 tablespoon Worcestershire sauce
1 cup finely chopped onion
½ cup sugar
Salt and pepper to taste

Wash spinach well; drain and tear into pieces. Place in large salad bowl. Add walnuts, bacon, eggs, mushrooms, tomatoes and bean sprouts. To prepare dressing, combine remaining ingredients and beat well with wire whisk. Pour on salad just before serving and toss. Serves 8.

Italian Bread with Garlic Butter

1 loaf Italian bread
½ cup butter, melted

Garlic salt
Parmesan cheese, grated

Cut Italian bread lengthwise. Coat split surfaces of bread with melted butter. Sprinkle garlic salt over buttered bread; top each half with a generous portion of grated Parmesan cheese. Bake uncovered at 350° for 15-20 minutes until lightly browned. Serves 8.

Mocha Almond Parfaits

1 quart coffee ice cream, softened
1 2¼-ounce package slivered almonds
3 ⅞-ounce English toffee candy bars

½ cup chocolate syrup
1 cup whipping cream, whipped
8 maraschino cherries with stems

Spoon ¼ cup ice cream into each of eight 4-ounce chilled parfait glasses; freeze 30 minutes. Toast and chop almonds. Crush toffee bars. Layer ½ tablespoon each of almonds, candy and chocolate syrup. Repeat layers of ice cream, almonds, candy and chocolate. Cover and freeze until firm. Garnish each parfait with whipped cream and a cherry. Yield: 8 parfaits.

Enjoy this dinner before dealing the cards, but plan on serving the parfaits at the conclusion of play as the scores are tallied. For light, crunchy snacks to munch on during play, check the index for recipes for Pizza Popcorn, Herbettes or Triple Goodness. Don't forget a small gift or favor for the winning couple.

A Quiet Evening At Home

Serves 8

Red Beans and Rice
King's Inn Salad
French Cheese Bread
Ice Cream Crunch with Praline Sauce

Red Beans and Rice

3 bacon slices
2 15-ounce cans red kidney
  beans
1 large onion, chopped
½ cup chopped celery
1 bell pepper, chopped
2 tablespoons dried parsley
2 tablespoons ketchup

1½ teaspoons Worcestershire
   sauce
2 ounces chopped pimento
8 ounces tomato sauce
2 teaspoons chili powder
2 pounds Polska Kielbasa
  sausage
2 cups raw rice, cooked

Fry bacon and crumble into undrained beans. In bacon drippings, sauté vegetables. Cook until wilted but not brown, stirring frequently. Add beans and remaining ingredients, except for sausage and rice. Cover and simmer 30-45 minutes. Prepare sausage according to package directions; cut into 1-inch pieces. Just before serving, add sausage and heat through. Serve red beans over rice. Serves 8.

King's Inn Salad

¼ cup red wine vinegar
1 tablespoon water
1 tablespoon prepared mustard
½ tablespoon sugar
1 tablespoon fresh lemon juice

1 tablespoon thyme leaves
1 package French dressing mix
⅔ cup salad oil
8 servings of mixed salad greens

To prepare dressing, put all ingredients except oil and salad greens in a jar and shake vigorously. Add oil and shake again. Chill. Before serving, place salad greens in large bowl and toss with dressing to taste. A little of this dressing goes a long way. If available, Good Seasons Old Fashion French dressing mix is preferred. Dressing is also recommended as a marinade for mushrooms or other raw vegetables. Serves 8.

French Cheese Bread

1 medium onion, chopped
½ cup butter, melted
2 tablespoons poppy seeds
Dash of salt

1 loaf French bread
1 pound Swiss cheese,
thinly sliced

Sauté onion in butter until clear; add poppy seeds and salt. Cut French bread into ½-inch slices; do not cut through loaf. Place slice of Swiss cheese into each cut of bread. Pour butter mixture over loaf. Wrap in foil. Bake 30 minutes at 350°. Serves 8.

Ice Cream Crunch with Praline Sauce

4 cups Rice Chex cereal
¼ cup sugar
1 cup grated coconut
½ cup butter, melted
½ gallon vanilla ice cream,
softened

1 cup chopped pecans
1½ cups brown sugar, firmly
packed
⅔ cup light corn syrup
4 tablespoons butter
1 5-ounce can evaporated milk

Crush cereal; mix with sugar and coconut. Reserve ½ cup of cereal mixture. Put remaining mixture into well greased 9x13x2-inch dish. Drizzle melted butter over crust. Spread softened ice cream over crust. Sprinkle reserved cereal mixture and pecans over top of ice cream. Freeze at least 1 hour before serving. To prepare praline sauce, combine brown sugar, syrup and 4 tablespoons butter in saucepan. Heat until mixture boils. Remove from heat and allow to cool. When mixture is lukewarm, add evaporated milk and blend well. Sauce keeps well in refrigerator. To serve, cut crunch into 3-inch squares. Serve individual squares topped with warm praline sauce. Serves 12.

When planning a family meal, break the spaghetti routine with this traditional Southern menu that is sure to please all ages. Remember that any leftover Red Beans and Rice can be frozen to enjoy another day.

"Pretend You're at the Beach" Party

Serves 8

Uncle Earl's Seafood Gumbo
Cole Slaw
Crunchy Cornbread
Layered Brownie Supreme

Uncle Earl's Seafood Gumbo

3 pounds fresh shrimp	4 pieces fresh parsley, minced
½ gallon water	1 16-ounce can okra
Commercial crab boil mix	1 16-ounce can tomatoes
½ cup plain flour	1 6-ounce can tomato paste
½ cup oil	3 bay leaves
3 medium onions, finely chopped	¼ teaspoon thyme
	Salt and pepper to taste
½ stalk celery, chopped	1 pound crab meat
1 large bell pepper, chopped	1 pint oysters, optional
3 cloves garlic, minced	4 cups cooked rice

Wash shrimp. Season ½ gallon of water with commercial crab boil; bring to a boil. Add shrimp and boil 5-10 minutes. Let shrimp stand in water for 10 minutes. Drain and peel shrimp, reserving stock. Combine flour and oil in heavy skillet; stir constantly over medium low heat until roux is dark brown. Be careful not to scorch. Cook chopped vegetables, garlic and parsley in roux until tender. Stir in okra, tomatoes, tomato paste, bay leaves, thyme, salt and pepper. In large pot, combine vegetable mixture and shrimp stock. Cook over medium heat for at least 1 hour. A few minutes before serving, add shrimp, crab meat and oysters, if desired. Serve hot in bowl topped with ⅓ cup of cooked rice per serving. Omit oysters if you wish to freeze gumbo. Serves 8-10.

Cole Slaw

1 large head cabbage, shredded	1 cup apple cider vinegar
2 carrots, grated	1 teaspoon dry mustard
1 large bell pepper, chopped	1 teaspoon celery seeds
½ cup sugar	1 tablespoon salt
¾ cup oil	

Place shredded cabbage in very large bowl. Layer carrots and bell pepper on top of cabbage. Sprinkle sugar over top of vegetables. Do not stir. Place remaining ingredients in saucepan and bring to a boil. Pour hot liquid over vegetables. Do not stir. Refrigerate at least 8 hours. Stir well before serving. Serves 8.

Crunchy Cornbread

3 eggs, beaten
8 ounces sour cream
1 8-ounce can corn, drained

1 tablespoon sugar
1 cup self-rising cornmeal
½ cup oil

Mix eggs, sour cream, corn and sugar. Add cornmeal and oil; mix well. Pour into greased 9-inch square baking pan. Bake at 375° for 45 minutes. Serves 8-10.

Layered Brownie Supreme

1 21.5-ounce package fudge
   brownie mix
1 pint chocolate chip ice cream,
   softened
1 pint Heavenly Hash ice cream,
   softened

12 ounces non-dairy whipped
    topping
1 cup slivered almonds,
   toasted

Prepare brownie mix according to package directions. Bake in greased 9x13x2-inch baking pan at 350° for 30 minutes. Cool brownie completely. Cut brownie crosswise into 3 9x4⅓-inch pieces. Place one brownie piece in bottom of loaf pan. Spoon chocolate chip ice cream on top and spread evenly. Top with second brownie piece. Spoon Heavenly Hash ice cream on top and spread evenly. Place remaining brownie piece on ice cream. Freeze brownie and ice cream layers for several hours or overnight, until ice cream refreezes. Unmold onto serving platter. Ice top and sides with whipped topping. Garnish top and sides with almonds. Serves 8-10.

When the winter winds howl and you wish you were at the sunny shore, invite friends over for this hearty seafood gumbo. Instead of place cards, have sun visors with each guest's name on it as a reminder that summer is around the corner. Be sure to have plenty of your favorite beach music on hand for the evening.

St. Patrick's Day Dinner

Serves 8

Janie's Beef Brisket
Cheddar Hash Brown Bake
Broccoli with Orange Sauce
Sally Lunn Squares
Hershey Bar Pie

Janie's Beef Brisket

1 4-pound beef brisket
Sliced onions
¼ cup chili sauce
12 ounces beer

2 tablespoons brown sugar
1 clove garlic, minced
2 tablespoons plain flour

Place brisket in 13x9-inch baking pan and cover with sliced onions. Combine all remaining ingredients except flour and pour over meat and onions. Cover pan with foil. Cook for 3½ hours at 350°. Remove foil and cook for an additional 30 minutes. Remove brisket from pan; add flour to pan drippings to make gravy. If mixture is too thick, add water until gravy reaches desired consistency. Before serving, slice brisket and top each serving with gravy. Serves 8.

Cheddar Hash Brown Bake

½ cup chopped onion
1 10½-ounce can potato soup
8 ounces sour cream
4 cups frozen shredded hash browns

8 ounces cheddar cheese, grated
Salt to taste

Mix all ingredients together except one-half grated cheese and pour into buttered 2-quart baking dish. Cover and bake at 350° for 1 hour. Uncover, sprinkle with remaining cheese and return to oven to melt. Serves 8.

Broccoli with Orange Sauce

2 tablespoons butter
2 tablespoons plain flour
1 cup orange juice
2 teaspoons sugar

⅛ teaspoon salt
Paprika
1 large bunch fresh broccoli

Melt butter in small saucepan. Stir in flour and cook until bubbly. Stirring constantly, add remaining ingredients except paprika and broccoli. Cook sauce until thickened and smooth. Steam broccoli and remove to serving platter. Before serving, top broccoli with sauce and sprinkle with paprika. Serves 8.

Sally Lunn Squares

½ cup shortening
½ cup sugar
3 eggs
2 cups flour, sifted

3 teaspoons baking powder
¾ teaspoon salt
1 cup milk

Cream shortening and sugar together until fluffy. Beat in eggs 1 at a time. Sift together flour, baking powder and salt. Add to egg mixture alternately with milk. Bake in a greased 9x9x2-inch glass dish at 425° for 30 minutes. Cut in squares and serve immediately with plenty of butter. Serves 8.

Hershey Bar Pie

1⅓ cups uncooked quick oats
½ cup finely chopped pecans
⅓ cup brown sugar, firmly
   packed
½ cup butter, melted

16 regular marshmallows
5 1.5-ounce milk chocolate bars
½ cup milk
10 ounces frozen whipped
   topping

To make pie shell, combine first 4 ingredients; cover bottom and sides of an 8-inch pie pan. Set aside. To make pie filling, combine marshmallows, chocolate bars and milk in double boiler. Cook over boiling water until marshmallows and candy have melted. Let cool. Stir whipped topping into cooled chocolate mixture and pour into pie shell. Chill at least 6 hours before serving. Serves 8.

Whether you're Irish or not, St. Patrick's Day is an ideal time for entertaining. Decorations such as shamrocks, pipes, bowlers, green confetti and balloons make it very easy to carry out your theme. To keep those Irish eyes smiling, end the meal with your favorite recipe of Irish coffee.

Woman on the Run Dinner Party

Serves 6

Boursin
Golden Flounder Fillets
Onion Pie
Low Country Citrus Salad with Poppy Seed Dressing
Spinach Cornbread Puff
Courtside Ice Cream Pie

Boursin

½ pound whipped butter
16 ounces cream cheese
⅛ teaspoon basil leaves
⅛ teaspoon garlic powder
⅛ teaspoon marjoram
⅛ teaspoon savory

⅛ teaspoon tarragon leaves
⅛ teaspoon paprika
⅛ teaspoon dill weed
⅛ teaspoon oregano leaves
⅛ teaspoon thyme
⅛ teaspoon parsley flakes

In a large bowl cream butter and cream cheese. Add herbs; blend well. Serve on crisp crackers. Yield: 2½ cups.

Golden Flounder Fillets

3 pounds flounder fillets
½ cup mayonnaise
1 teaspoon grated onion
¼ teaspoon hot sauce

1 cup Parmesan cheese
Paprika
Lemon slices
Fresh parsley sprigs

Broil fillets for 3 minutes. Mix together mayonnaise, onion, hot sauce, and Parmesan cheese. Top fillets with mayonnaise mixture and sprinkle with paprika. Broil for 4 minutes. To serve, garnish with lemon slices and parsley. Serves 6.

Onion Pie

1 cup salted cracker crumbs
6 tablespoons butter, melted
*2 large white onions, thinly
    sliced*
2 tablespoons butter
¾ cup milk

2 eggs, beaten
¾ teaspoon salt
⅛ teaspoon pepper
½ teaspoon Italian seasoning
*¾ cup grated sharp cheddar
    cheese*

Mix cracker crumbs and melted butter. Press onto 8-inch pie plate covering bottom and sides. Sauté onions in butter until tender, then place on crust. Mix milk, eggs, salt, pepper and seasoning; pour over onions. Sprinkle cheese over top. Bake at 350° for 30 minutes. Serves 6.

Low Country Citrus Salad with Poppy Seed Dressing

½ cup salad oil
¼ cup vinegar
¼ cup ketchup
1 teaspoon grated onion
1 teaspoon paprika
½ teaspoon salt

¼ cup sugar
1½ teaspoons poppy seeds
Mixed salad greens
2 grapefruit, seeded and sectioned
2 avocados, peeled and sliced

To prepare dressing, blend all ingredients, except mixed salad greens and fruit. Refrigerate for at least 2 hours. To serve, arrange grapefruit and avocado on bed of mixed greens and top with dressing. Serves 6.

Spinach Cornbread Puff

10½ ounces frozen chopped spinach
1 7-ounce box cornbread mix
4 eggs, beaten

6 tablespoons butter, melted
1 medium onion, chopped
8 ounces cottage cheese
½ teaspoon salt

Thaw spinach and squeeze out all the water. Combine spinach and all remaining ingredients. Stir just until moistened. Pour into greased 9-inch pie plate. Bake at 400° for 25 minutes or until lightly browned. Serves 6.

Courtside Ice Cream Pie

2 cups crushed Oreo cookies
¼ cup butter, melted
1 5-ounce can evaporated milk
2 tablespoons butter
½ cup sugar
2 ounces semi-sweet chocolate

½ teaspoon vanilla extract
1 quart vanilla ice cream, softened
8 ounces frozen whipped topping

Mix the cookie crumbs and melted butter; press into 2 8-inch pie plates. Heat milk, butter, sugar and chocolate; stir until thickened. Add vanilla; stir and let cool. Spread softened ice cream over crust. Spoon chocolate sauce over ice cream. Place pie in freezer until ready to serve. Remove and ice with whipped topping. Yield: 2 pies.

"Woman on the Run" has come to have multiple meanings in Greenville in recent years. While many women stay "on the run" with careers, families, and community, they are adding the dimension of health to their priorities. An annual Greenville event that celebrates wellness is the prestigious "Women on the Run" race which has drawn more than 1,000 women from the collegiate to the national levels for its one, three and five mile races. Greenville's race is fourth in a series of "Women on the Run" races held throughout the country.

"Take Me Out to the Ballgame" Supper

Serves 6

Hot Zucchini Bites
Linguine Con Pollo
Marinated Vegetables with Salad Greens
Commercial Hard Rolls
Devil's Chocolate Cheesecake

Hot Zucchini Bites

3 cups zucchini, peeled and
  thinly sliced
1 cup commercial dry biscuit
  mix
½ cup finely chopped onion
½ cup fresh grated Parmesan
  cheese
½ cup grated mozzarella cheese
2 tablespoons chopped fresh
  parsley

½ teaspoon salt
⅛ teaspoon pepper
½ teaspoon oregano
½ teaspoon seasoning salt
1 clove garlic, finely chopped
4 large eggs, beaten
¼ pound fresh mushrooms,
  sliced

Preheat oven to 350°. Lightly grease 9x13x2-inch baking dish. Mix all
ingredients and pour into prepared dish. Bake 25 minutes or until golden
brown. Cut into 1½-inch squares and serve warm. Yield: 48 appetizers.

Linguine Con Pollo

1½ pounds boneless chicken
  breasts
1 pound fresh asparagus spears
¾ pound linguine
2 tablespoons butter
  Salt and pepper to taste
4 tablespoons chopped green
  onions
1 cup whipping cream

1 dried hot red pepper,
  crumbled
⅛ teaspoon freshly grated
  nutmeg
¼ pound Gorgonzola cheese
2 tablespoons chopped fresh
  tarragon
½ cup freshly grated Parmesan
  cheese

Remove skin, sinew and cartilage from chicken breasts. Cut chicken into
1½x½-inch strips. Scrape and trim asparagus; cut off and discard tough
ends. Cut asparagus on diagonal into 1½-inch lengths. Drop asparagus
pieces into boiling water and drain; set aside. Cook pasta according to
package directions. Melt butter in large saucepan. Add chicken strips and
cook 30 seconds, or until chicken changes color, stirring constantly. Stir in
salt, pepper and asparagus. Add onion and cook 30 seconds. Stir in cream,

continued

hot pepper and nutmeg. Break Gorgonzola cheese into small pieces and add to pan. Cook until cheese melts. Stir in tarragon. Drain pasta and add to sauce. Toss well. Sprinkle Parmesan cheese over individual servings. Serve immediately. Serves 6.

Marinated Vegetables with Salad Greens

1 cup vinegar
½ cup oil
1 clove garlic
1½ tablespoons salt
½ tablespoon fresh ground pepper
1 teaspoon oregano
1 tablespoon dried parsley flakes
1 onion, sliced in rings

1 pint cherry tomatoes
½ pound fresh mushrooms, sliced
1 3¼-ounce can pitted ripe olives, drained and sliced
2 14-ounce cans artichoke hearts, drained and quartered
1 small head lettuce
½ pound fresh spinach

Combine vinegar, oil, garlic, salt, pepper, oregano, parsley and onion; mix well. Pour over tomatoes, mushrooms, olives and artichoke hearts. Cover and refrigerate overnight. To serve, arrange salad greens on individual plates. Top with marinated vegetables. Serves 6.

Devil's Chocolate Cheesecake

¾ cup graham cracker crumbs
5 tablespoons butter, melted
2 tablespoons sugar
1 ounce semi-sweet chocolate, grated
3 eggs
1 cup sugar
24 ounces cream cheese, softened

12 ounces semi-sweet chocolate
8 ounces sour cream
¾ cup unsalted butter
1 teaspoon vanilla extract
1 cup coarsely chopped pecans
Whipped cream

Combine graham cracker crumbs, butter, 2 tablespoons sugar and 1 ounce grated chocolate. Press mixture firmly into bottom of 8-inch springform pan. Beat eggs with 1 cup sugar until thickened. In separate bowl, beat cream cheese until soft. Add cheese to egg mixture; beat well. In top of double boiler, combine remaining chocolate, sour cream, butter and vanilla; heat until chocolate melts. Stir chocolate into cheese mixture and fold in pecans. Pour batter into pan and bake at 325° for 2 hours or until center is firm. Let cake cool on wire rack. Chill 12 hours. Serve with whipped cream. Serves 8.

Baseball fans in Greenville find plenty to cheer about at the fast-paced Greenville Braves AA home games. The city built the Municipal Stadium for the "G-Braves" in 1984 on Mauldin Road near I-85. Area fans also travel I-85 to Atlanta to watch major league Braves baseball.

Uptown Blue Jean Sitdown

Serves 12

Country Shrimp Boil
Tossed Green Salad with Peggy's Roquefort Dressing
Hush Puppies
Milky Way Ice Cream
Shortbread Cookies

Country Shrimp Boil

⅓ cup powdered seafood boil
1 lemon, sliced
3 pounds smoked sausage
12 ears of corn, broken into halves

5 pounds medium shrimp, unpeeled
Cocktail sauce
Dijon-style mustard

Fill a very large pot with water; add powdered seafood boil and lemon. Bring to a boil. Cut sausage into 2-inch pieces; add to boiling water and cook for 5 minutes. Add corn and continue to boil for 10 minutes. Stir in shrimp and continue cooking for 3-5 minutes. Drain. Serve with cocktail sauce and Dijon-style mustard. Serves 12.

Tossed Green Salad with Peggy's Roquefort Dressing

Mixed salad greens
8 ounces Roquefort cheese, crumbled
1 cup oil
½ cup vinegar

1 teaspoon Worcestershire sauce
1 tablespoon sugar
Salt and pepper to taste

Wash and tear salad greens. Refrigerate until ready to serve. To prepare dressing, crumble cheese by hand. Combine remaining ingredients. Stir in cheese. Do not use blender. Immediately before serving, toss salad greens with dressing. This dressing is also delicious served over chilled grapefruit. Yield: 2½ cups.

Hush Puppies

2 cups yellow cornmeal
1 cup self-rising flour
½ cup sugar
½ teaspoon baking powder
2 teaspoons salt

1 cup buttermilk
4 eggs
Whole milk, if needed
Oil for frying

Combine all ingredients except milk and oil in large mixing bowl. Mixture should be firm but not dry. If dry, add small amount of whole milk. Heat oil in deep fryer until very hot (375°). Drop teaspoonfuls of batter into hot oil; cook only a few at a time, turning once. Fry 3-5 minutes or until golden. Drain on paper towels. Yield: 48 hush puppies.

Milky Way Ice Cream

12 1¾-ounce Milky Way bars
1 14-ounce can condensed milk
3 quarts milk

1 15.5-ounce can chocolate syrup

Break up candy bars. Melt over low heat and add condensed milk; stir constantly. Let cool and stir occasionally. Add 1 quart milk and beat until well blended. Pour mixture into container of electric ice cream churn. Stir in chocolate syrup and enough of remaining milk until mixture is 4 inches from top. Freeze according to manufacturer's instructions. Yield: 1½ gallons ice cream.

Shortbread Cookies

1½ cups butter
1 cup powdered sugar
3 cups plain flour, sifted

½ teaspoon salt
½ teaspoon vanilla extract
¼ cup sugar

Cream butter and powdered sugar until smooth. Sift flour and salt together; add to butter mixture. Add vanilla; blend thoroughly. Wrap dough in waxed paper and chill until firm. Roll dough to ⅝-inch thickness and cut with 3-inch cookie cutter. Place cookies on ungreased cookie sheet; sprinkle with granulated sugar. Refrigerate for 20 minutes. Bake at 325° for 20 minutes. Cookies should not be brown around edges. Yield: 20 cookies.

This menu is a sure success for an informal evening, indoors or out. For tablecloths use newspapers and for napkins pass rolls of paper towels. Encourage everyone to come in blue jeans or their most comfortable attire. Enjoy a laid back evening that's fun and easy.

Freedom Weekend Cookout

Serves 6

Green Chili Dip
Grilled Beef Rollups
Tomato Potato Melt
Onion and Bell Pepper Casserole
Piquante Dressed Salad
Coffee Toffee Pie

Green Chili Dip

2 large tomatoes, peeled and chopped
1 4-ounce can chopped ripe olives
1 4-ounce can chopped green chilies
3 green onions, chopped

3 tablespoons olive oil
Tabasco to taste
Pepper to taste
1½ tablespoons white vinegar
1 teaspoon salt
1 teaspoon garlic salt

Mix ingredients. Chill 12-24 hours. Serve with corn chips. Yield: 1 cup.

Grilled Beef Rollups

2 0.6-ounce packages dry Italian dressing
Olive oil
Water
Red wine vinegar
3 pounds top round steak
Unseasoned meat tenderizer

2 teaspoons garlic salt
1 teaspoon freshly ground pepper
1 pound bacon, partially cooked
4 tablespoons dried parsley
½ teaspoon dried tarragon

Prepare Italian dressing according to directions, using olive oil, water and red wine vinegar. Pound steak to even thickness, about ½ inch. Use tenderizer according to directions. Sprinkle meat with garlic salt and pepper. Place partially cooked bacon lengthwise on top of steak. Combine parsley and tarragon and sprinkle over bacon. Roll up meat beginning at narrow end. Secure with toothpicks at 1-inch intervals. Cut into 1-inch thick slices using serrated knife. Marinate in Italian dressing for 24-36 hours, turning meat several times. Grill over medium coals until desired doneness. Serves 6.

Tomato Potato Melt

5 large baking potatoes
¾ cup butter, softened
9 bacon slices, cooked and crumbled
3 small tomatoes, diced

2 green onions with tops, minced
2 cups grated cheddar cheese
Salt and pepper to taste

Bake potatoes in 400° oven for 1 hour. Cool slightly. Cut in half lengthwise. Scoop out pulp into mixing bowl, reserving shells. Mash potatoes. Add butter to mashed potatoes; blend. Add remaining ingredients to potato mixture. Stuff mixture into potato skins and bake at 350° until cheese melts. Serves 10.

Onion and Bell Pepper Casserole

8 medium white onions, peeled
3 large bell peppers
4 tablespoons butter
4 tablespoons plain flour
1½ cups milk

1 teaspoon salt
⅛ teaspoon pepper
4 tablespoons grated Parmesan cheese
¾ cup buttered bread crumbs

Cook whole onions in boiling salted water until tender. Drain, cut in half and place in buttered 9x13x2-inch baking dish. Set aside. Cut bell peppers into strips. Melt butter in skillet. Add peppers and sauté until softened. Stir in flour to make paste. Add milk and cook until thickened. Season with salt and pepper; add cheese. Pour peppers over onions and cover with buttered bread crumbs. Bake at 350° for 20-30 minutes until hot and bubbly. Serves 6.

Piquante Dressed Salad

½ cup vinegar
2 teaspoons salt
1 teaspoon sugar
½ teaspoon pepper
1 teaspoon paprika
1½ teaspoons dry mustard
1½ cups salad oil

1 teaspoon prepared mustard
1 teaspoon Worcestershire sauce
8 drops hot sauce
¼ onion
Assorted salad greens

Combine first 6 ingredients in quart jar. Shake well. Add next four ingredients; shake again. Leave onion in jar to season; discard before serving. Best prepared day before serving. Refrigerate until ready to serve. Shake well before serving over greens. Yield: 2 cups dressing.

Coffee Toffee Pie

1½ cups unsifted plain flour
6 tablespoons butter, melted
¼ cup brown sugar, firmly packed
¾ cup finely chopped pecans
1 ounce unsweetened chocolate, grated
1 teaspoon vanilla extract
1 tablespoon water
¾ cup butter, softened
1 cup sugar
1½ ounces unsweetened chocolate
1 tablespoon instant coffee granules
3 eggs
2 cups whipping cream, whipped
½ cup powdered sugar
2 tablespoons instant coffee granules
2 tablespoons coffee liqueur
Chocolate curls for garnish

Butter two 10-inch pie plates. Combine flour, melted butter, brown sugar, pecans, 1 ounce grated chocolate, vanilla and water. Mix well and put half of mixture into each plate. Press onto bottom and sides. Bake 15 minutes at 350°. Cool completely. Cream remaining butter. Gradually add sugar, beating until light and lemon colored. Melt remaining chocolate; allow to cool slightly and add to butter mixture. Stir in 1 tablespoon coffee granules. Add eggs, one at a time, beating well after each addition. Pour filling into cooled pie shells. Cover and refrigerate overnight. Whip cream with powdered sugar, remaining coffee granules and coffee liqueur. Spread over filling and garnish with chocolate curls. Yield: 2 pies.

The weekend of July 4th in Greenville is noted for color and excitement as hot air balloons fill the skies. Greenville is host to Freedom Weekend Aloft, a four-day event of hot air balloon races and competitions that draw as many as 250 balloonists from all over the country. Added attractions such as concerts, firework displays and at least one spectacular mass ascension of hot air balloons draws over 100,000 spectators to America's second largest balloon festival.

Labor Day Poolside Buffet

Serves 16

Crowd Appeaser
Garden Dip
Tony's Grilled Shrimp
Baddest Ribs in Town
Bacon Swiss Tossed Salad
Parmesan Corn on the Grill
Commercial Sourdough Rolls
Churned Vanilla Ice Cream
Chocolate Chip Caramel Chews

Crowd Appeaser

1 cup butter	4 cups Corn Chex cereal
2½ teaspoons garlic salt	4 cups peanuts
3 tablespoons Worcestershire sauce	4 cups pretzels
4 cups Honey Comb cereal	4 cups cheese crackers

Melt butter in roasting pan; add garlic salt and Worcestershire sauce. Stir in remaining ingredients, mixing until well coated. Cook at 250° for 1 hour, stirring every 15 minutes. May be made ahead and stored in airtight container until needed. Mixture freezes well. Yield: 20 cups.

Garden Dip

1 8-ounce can water chestnuts	1 tablespoon minced onion
10 ounces frozen chopped spinach	1 0.4-ounce envelope buttermilk dressing
1 cup sour cream	Corn chips
2 tablespoons mayonnaise	

Chop water chestnuts. Thaw spinach and drain thoroughly. Mix all ingredients. Serve with corn chips. Yield: 2½ cups.

Tony's Grilled Shrimp

2 cups olive oil
½ cup soy sauce
1 cup red wine
4 tablespoons lemon juice
½ cup dried parsley
6 tablespoons tarragon
8 pounds raw shrimp

2 pounds butter
8 tablespoons soy sauce
8 tablespoons Worcestershire sauce
2 teaspoons garlic powder
Hot sauce to taste

To prepare marinade, combine olive oil, soy sauce, red wine, lemon juice, parsley and tarragon. Cut open each shrimp's back with shears and drop into marinade. Shrimp should marinate in refrigerator all day, stirring occasionally. When ready to cook, use mesh over grill to prevent shrimp from falling into coals. Grill drained shrimp over medium heat, turning several times until they turn pink. Combine remaining ingredients and heat. Serve shrimp with garlic butter sauce. Serves 16.

Baddest Ribs in Town

1 cup vinegar
2 cups water
½ cup sugar
4 tablespoons prepared mustard
2 teaspoons pepper
2 tablespoons salt
1 teaspoon cayenne pepper
2 large lemons, cut in thick slices

2 medium onions, cut in thick slices
1 cup butter
2 cups ketchup
½ cup Worcestershire sauce
16 pounds spareribs

Prepare sauce by combining all ingredients except ribs, ketchup and Worcestershire sauce in a large saucepan. Simmer 20 minutes. Add ketchup and Worcestershire sauce and bring to boil. Slice spareribs into individual ribs. In large pot, parboil ribs in water with 2 cups barbecue sauce for 25-30 minutes. Arrange drained ribs on roasting pan meat side up; pour remaining sauce over ribs and cover with aluminum foil. Bake at 180° for 7-9 hours. Uncover and bake 1½ hours. Serves 16.

Bacon Swiss Tossed Salad

1 cup mayonnaise
Juice of 2 lemons
1 medium onion, finely minced
4 cups frozen peas
2 cups Swiss cheese strips

Salt and pepper to taste
6 cups torn lettuce
1 pound bacon, cooked and crumbled

Twenty-four hours before serving, combine mayonnaise, lemon juice and onion in bowl. Cut cheese into thin strips. Add cheese and frozen peas. Stir well; add salt and pepper. Cover and refrigerate. Before serving, add lettuce and bacon; toss well. Serves 16.

Parmesan Corn on the Grill

16 ears fresh corn
1 cup butter, softened
1 cup grated Parmesan cheese

2 tablespoons dried parsley
½ teaspoon salt

Remove husks and silks from corn. Combine butter, cheese, parsley and salt; stir well. Spread mixture on corn and place each ear on a piece of aluminum foil; wrap tightly. Grill corn over medium coals 20-30 minutes, turning several times. Serves 16.

Churned Vanilla Ice Cream

6 eggs
3 cups sugar
4 cups half-and-half

2 tablespoons vanilla extract
Whole milk

Beat eggs. Gradually add sugar, beating well. Pour mixture into freezer can. Add half-and-half, vanilla and enough whole milk to reach fill line. Churn until firm. Recipe can be made using only whole milk. Yield: 1 gallon.

Chocolate Chip Caramel Chews

2¾ cups sifted plain flour
2½ teaspoons baking powder
¼ teaspoon salt
1 pound light brown sugar
1⅓ sticks margarine

3 eggs, lightly beaten
1 cup chopped pecans
12 ounces semi-sweet chocolate chips
1 teaspoon vanilla extract

Sift together flour, baking powder and salt. Cream sugar and margarine, and combine with flour mixture. Add eggs; mix well. Add nuts, chocolate chips and vanilla. Spread mixture in 15½x10½x1-inch greased pan and bake at 325° for 45 minutes. Cut into 1x2-inch bars. Yield: 72 bars.

For this outdoor party try substituting terry cloth finger towels for napkins. They will be colorful yet provide the absorbency needed for these particular dishes. Disposable utensils and plates will make clean-up quick and easy. Don't forget to set out attractive insect repellant candles to ward off any uninvited guests.

Half Time Supper

Serves 12

North Alabama Barbecued Chicken
Hoppin' John
Baked Vegetable Medley
Bread with Herbed Butter
Peanut Butter Cheesecake

North Alabama Barbecued Chicken

6 small fryers
  Salt and pepper to taste
  Red pepper to taste
2 quarts white vinegar
1 cup butter, melted

3 cups mayonnaise
4 cups white vinegar
½ cup pepper
  Hickory chips, soaked in water

Wash fryers thoroughly and sprinkle with salt, pepper and red pepper. Combine vinegar and butter. Marinate fryers overnight in vinegar mixture. When ready to cook, start charcoal fire and place fryers in covered container in a 350° oven for 30 minutes. Prepare white sauce by combining mayonnaise, vinegar and pepper; shake. Store in refrigerator. When coals turn white, add hickory chips to fire and place chicken on grill away from direct heat. Cook with grill cover down for 2½ hours or until tender. Baste frequently with marinade. If grill does not have a cover, cook for a shorter time, basting frequently. Remove chicken to platter. Serve with white sauce. Serves 12.

Hoppin' John

1 pound dry field peas
1 teaspoon sugar
2 cups raw rice
3 bacon slices, chopped

1 medium onion, chopped
2¼ cups broth from peas
  Salt and pepper to taste

Wash and cull peas. Place peas in pot; cover with water and soak overnight. Bring peas to boil; reduce heat and cook until tender. Add sugar. Wash rice thoroughly. In 2-quart pan, fry bacon; add onion and sauté until tender. Add broth, raw rice, and peas; season to taste. Bring to a boil. Cover and simmer 20 minutes without stirring. Stir well before serving. Serves 12.

Baked Vegetable Medley

4 large yellow squash	Salt and pepper to taste
8 large tomatoes	Butter
4 large zucchini	Parmesan cheese, grated
6 medium white onions	1 cup grated mozzarella cheese

Grease two 2-quart deep dish casseroles. Wash squash; slice thinly. Put one layer of yellow squash in each casserole. Sprinkle with salt and pepper. Dot with butter and sprinkle with Parmesan cheese. Repeat process with layer of tomatoes, leaving the skin on tomatoes. Repeat again with layer of zucchini and then with layer of onions. Repeat layers until casserole dishes are completely filled. Bake at 325° for 45 minutes. Sprinkle top with mozzarella cheese and bake for 5 additional minutes. Serves 12.

Bread with Herbed Butter

1 loaf French bread	1 tablespoon chopped chives
¾ cup butter	½ teaspoon dried basil
1 tablespoon parsley	¼ teaspoon lemon juice

Cut French bread into 1-inch slices. Combine remaining ingredients, mixing well. Spread butter mixture between bread slices. Wrap loaf in foil; bake at 350° for 30 minutes. Serves 12.

Peanut Butter Cheesecake

1 cup graham cracker crumbs	2 tablespoons butter, melted
¼ cup brown sugar, firmly packed	2 teaspoons vanilla extract
¼ cup butter, melted	1½ cups whipping cream
2 cups creamy peanut butter	4 ounces semi-sweet chocolate
2 cups sugar	3 tablespoons hot coffee
16 ounces cream cheese, softened	

Combine crumbs, brown sugar and ¼ cup butter. Press into bottom and halfway up sides of 9-inch springform pan. Beat peanut butter, sugar, cream cheese, 2 tablespoons butter and vanilla in large bowl until smooth and creamy. Whip cream until soft peaks form. Fold whipped cream into peanut butter mixture. Spoon into crust. Refrigerate for 6 hours. Melt chocolate with coffee in double boiler over simmering water. Spread over filling. Refrigerate until firm. Serves 12.

Don't be a football widow! Even if you don't enjoy football, create your own fun by entertaining friends with this home-cooked creole. The creole and cheesecake can be prepared ahead of time, leaving plenty of time to spend with your guests.

Monday Night Football Supper

Serves 12

Mushrooms Stuffed with Clams
Carolina Creole
Green Salad with Romano Dressing
Buttered Beer Loaf
Amaretto Cheesecake

Mushrooms Stuffed with Clams

1½ pounds large mushrooms
   Fresh lemon juice
6 tablespoons butter
3 medium onions, finely
   chopped
3 cloves garlic
3 teaspoons dried oregano

¾ cup chopped dried parsley
   Salt and pepper to taste
4½ tablespoons plain flour
2 6½-ounce cans minced clams
1½ cups dry bread crumbs
   Parmesan cheese, grated

Preheat oven to 400°. Remove stems from mushrooms; chop stems finely. Sprinkle lemon juice over mushroom caps. Melt butter in skillet and sauté onion and garlic; remove garlic. Add oregano, parsley, chopped mushroom stems, salt and pepper. Stir in flour and juice from one can of clams. Drain other can of clams; discarding liquid. Add clams and bread crumbs to onion mixture. Stuff mushroom caps and sprinkle generously with Parmesan cheese. Bake at 400° for 30 minutes or until bubbly. Serve as appetizer. Serves 12.

Carolina Creole

½ pound mild bulk sausage
1 large bell pepper, chopped
1 large onion, chopped
2 stalks celery, chopped
1 28-ounce can whole tomatoes
1 6-ounce can tomato paste
1 4-ounce can mushroom pieces
1 32-ounce jar spaghetti sauce

⅛ cup sugar
½ teaspoon salt
¼ teaspoon pepper
½ cup dry white wine
4 pounds shrimp, cooked and
   peeled
2 cups rice, cooked

Brown sausage in skillet; remove sausage and drain. In the drippings, sauté pepper, onion and celery; add to sausage and put into 8-quart Dutch oven. Mash whole tomatoes; add tomatoes and juice to sausage mixture. Stir in remaining ingredients except for wine, shrimp and rice. Simmer for 1 hour, stirring occasionally. Remove from heat. Before serving, add wine and heat slowly until bubbly. Add shrimp and cook until heated through. Serve over cooked rice. Serves 12.

Green Salad with Romano Dressing

1 cup grated Romano cheese
⅔ cup oil
3 tablespoons olive oil
Juice of 1 lemon
1 clove garlic
1 head iceberg lettuce
1 head bibb or red leaf lettuce
½ bunch broccoli, cut into
    florets

2 fresh tomatoes, cut into
    wedges
1 cucumber, thinly sliced
3 green onions with tops,
    chopped
¼ cup sesame seeds, toasted

Combine cheese, oils, lemon juice and garlic in small bowl; stir well. Chill overnight. Remove garlic. Pour mixture into blender container; blend well. Place prepared salad greens and vegetables in large salad bowl. When ready to serve, pour dressing over salad and sprinkle with sesame seeds. Toss and serve immediately. Serves 12.

Buttered Beer Loaf

6 cups self-rising flour
6 tablespoons sugar

2 12-ounce cans cold beer
1 cup butter, melted

Combine flour, sugar and beer; mix well. Pour into two greased 9x5-inch loaf pans. Bake at 350° for 30 minutes. Pour butter over top and cook for additional 10 minutes, or until lightly browned. Serve warm. Yield: 2 loaves.

Amaretto Cheesecake

1½ cups graham cracker crumbs
2 tablespoons sugar
1 teaspoon cinnamon
6 tablespoons butter, melted
24 ounces cream cheese,
    softened
1 cup sugar

4 eggs
⅓ cup Amaretto
8 ounces sour cream
4 teaspoons sugar
1 tablespoon Amaretto
¼ cup sliced toasted almonds
1 1.2-ounce chocolate candy bar

Combine graham cracker crumbs, 2 tablespoons sugar, cinnamon, and melted butter. Mix well. Firmly press mixture into bottom and ½ inch up the sides of 9-inch springform pan. Beat cream cheese with electric mixer until light and fluffy. Gradually add 1 cup sugar, mixing well. Add eggs, one at a time, beating well after each addition. Stir in ⅓ cup Amaretto. Pour into prepared pan. Bake at 375° for 45 to 50 minutes or until set. Combine sour cream, 4 teaspoons sugar, and 1 tablespoon Amaretto. Stir well and spoon over the cheesecake. Bake at 500° for 5 minutes. Let cool to room temperature; then refrigerate for 24 to 48 hours. Cheesecake is best when thoroughly chilled and flavors have time to ripen. Garnish with almonds and grated chocolate. Serves 12-18.

After the Zoo Cookout

Serves 12

My Favorite Snack
French Style Pizza
Tempting Taste Tossed Salad
Layered Brickle Ice Cream Squares

My Favorite Snack

9 tablespoons butter
1½ tablespoons Worcestershire
   sauce
½ cup grated Parmesan cheese
4½ cups Corn Chex cereal

4½ ounces canned potato sticks
18 ounces mixed nuts
8 ounces sesame seeds
8 ounces sunflower seeds

Melt butter in large skillet; add Worcestershire sauce and Parmesan cheese; mix well. Add dry ingredients and toss until well-coated. Spread on an ungreased baking sheet. Bake at 350° for 15 minutes; stirring twice. Watch carefully, as mixture burns easily. Drain on paper towels. Cool and store in airtight containers. Yield: 9 cups.

French Style Pizza

1½ packages frozen puff pastry
   sheets
3 tablespoons butter
¾ cup chopped onion
2 cups tomato sauce
1½ teaspoons oregano
2 egg yolks

2 teaspoons water
48 thin slices pepperoni
1½ pounds ground beef, browned
18 ounces shaved ham, optional
18 ounces mozzarella cheese,
   grated

Thaw pastry for 30 minutes. Melt butter and sauté onion until clear. Stir in sauce and oregano; simmer 5 minutes. Cool slightly. Place egg yolks in small bowl; beat with water; set aside. Place pastry sheets on lightly floured surface and roll each sheet into a 16x9-inch rectangle. Cut each rectangle into 2 strips, one 16x5-inch and one 16x4-inch. Place each 16x4-inch strip on heavy cookie sheet, and brush edges with the egg wash. Spoon half of tomato sauce down the center of each strip, leaving one inch all around. Arrange pepperoni slices on top of sauce. Sprinkle ground beef and ham, if desired, on top of pepperoni. Sprinkle with grated cheese. Carefully place each 16x5-inch strip of pastry on top, pressing edges down firmly against bottom pastry. Crimp edges with a fork to seal. Brush top of each pizza with egg wash. Make four slits in top of each pizza and bake for 25 minutes at 425°. Can freeze before baking. Serves 12.

Tempting Taste Tossed Salad

2 medium heads lettuce	24 stuffed olives
6 tablespoons chopped fresh parsley	2 1.12-ounce packages meat marinade
6 green onions with tops, chopped	2 tablespoons water
4 stalks celery, chopped	⅔ cup oil
1 large bell pepper, cut into strips	4 tablespoons vinegar
4 tomatoes, sliced	2 tablespoons lemon juice
	1 teaspoon paprika
	Salt to taste

In serving bowl, tear lettuce into bite-size pieces. Add parsley, green onions, celery and bell pepper; toss well. Top with sliced tomatoes, then olives; set aside. Mix meat marinade, water, oil, vinegar and lemon juice in a bowl. Before serving, spoon over salad. Sprinkle with paprika and salt, then toss. Serves 12.

Layered Brickle Ice Cream Squares

2½ cups graham cracker crumbs	1½ cups sugar
6 tablespoons sugar	1 cup evaporated milk
⅔ cup butter, melted	⅛ teaspoon salt
1 gallon vanilla ice cream, softened	¼ cup butter
2 7.8-ounce bags brickle bits	¼ cup light corn syrup

Blend first 3 ingredients together and press into bottom and sides of a lightly greased 9x13x2-inch baking dish. Chill in refrigerator 30 minutes. Spoon half of the ice cream into prepared baking dish. Sprinkle with ¾ bag brickle bits. Heap with remaining ice cream and freeze. To prepare sauce, combine sugar, milk, salt, butter and syrup in saucepan. Bring to a boil over low heat. Boil 1 minute. Remove from heat and stir in remaining brickle bits. Cool, stirring occasionally; chill. When ready to serve, cut ice cream dessert into squares. Stir sauce well and spoon over individual dessert squares. Refrigerate remaining sauce for later use. Serves 12.

The Greenville Zoo had its meager beginnings in the 1960's with a few ducks and a buffalo. It has since grown to a 14-acre site in Cleveland Park, and is the home of more than 500 animals. Annually, more than 120,000 people stroll through Greenville's zoo, enjoying the lovely setting and observing the wide variety of animals. The zoo offers educational programs to school children and special interest groups throughout the year. These include summer Zoo Camp, tours of the zoo, and zoological classes.

"What To Do With All Those Birds"

Serves 8

Blue Cheese Vegetable Dip
Dove Bog
Hunters' Green Salad
Cornbread Carousel
Harvest Fruit Pie

Blue Cheese Vegetable Dip

1 cup sour cream
⅛ teaspoon garlic powder
½ teaspoon onion powder
½ teaspoon salt

¾ teaspoon paprika
4 tablespoons blue cheese
Dash of red pepper

Mix all ingredients together. Refrigerate for several hours before serving. Serve with assorted raw vegetables. Yield: 1¼ cups.

Dove Bog

3 medium onions, chopped
4 stalks celery, chopped
1 teaspoon salt
2 teaspoons pepper

10 dove breasts
5 pieces raw chicken
1½ pounds smoked sausage
2 cups raw rice

In 7-quart pot place onion, celery, salt, pepper, dove and chicken. Cover with water and boil covered about 45 minutes. Cut sausage into thick slices and add to pot. Continue cooking an additional 15 minutes. Remove dove, chicken and sausage; reserve broth. Debone chicken and dove. Cut into bite-size pieces. Measure broth, adding enough water, if necessary, to yield 4 cups. Return broth to pot, add rice and bring to boil. Cook on low 10 minutes. Add dove, chicken and sausage. Cook 10-15 minutes on medium, stirring occasionally. Can prepare ahead of time. Serves 8.

Hunters' Green Salad

1⅓ cups oil
½ cup vinegar
¼ cup grated Parmesan cheese
1 tablespoon sugar
2 teaspoons salt
1 teaspoon celery salt

½ teaspoon white pepper
½ teaspoon dry mustard
¼ teaspoon paprika
1 clove garlic, minced
Mixed salad greens
Fresh tomatoes

Prepare dressing by combining first 10 ingredients in jar and shaking well. Refrigerate dressing until ready to serve. To serve, mix greens and tomatoes in bowl. Toss with dressing. Serves 8.

Cornbread Carousel

3 cups cornmeal
1 cup plain flour
¾ cup sugar
1 teaspoon salt

1 teaspoon soda
1 teaspoon baking powder
½ cup shortening, melted
3 cups buttermilk

Combine all ingredients and mix well. Spoon into well-greased 10-inch tube pan; let stand 10 minutes. Bake at 350° for 1 hour or until done. Cool 5 minutes before removing from pan. Serves 12.

Harvest Fruit Pie

½ cup butter, softened
¾ cup sugar
2 eggs
½ cup flaked coconut
½ cup raisins

½ cup chopped nuts
1 teaspoon vinegar
1 9-inch pie shell, unbaked
1 cup whipping cream
1 tablespoon sherry

Mix butter and sugar. Add eggs and mix well. Blend in coconut, raisins, chopped nuts and vinegar. Pour into pie shell. Bake at 350° for 40 minutes or until firm. Whip cream and stir in sherry. Garnish each slice of pie with dollop of whipped cream. Serves 8.

This dinner is a good way to empty your freezer of last season's game to make way for the new. Since this is a good one-plate meal it is perfect for casually entertaining a crowd. Wrap your silverware in mix-and-match cloth napkins for a colorful touch.

Happy Hunter's Dinner

Serves 6

Honey Orange Duck
Jean's Oyster Stew
Wild Rice Casserole
Tomatoes Stuffed with Spinach
Special Pecan Pie

Honey Orange Duck

3	mallard ducks	9	tablespoons orange juice
7½	teaspoons salt	6	teaspoons lemon juice
3	teaspoons ginger	3	teaspoons orange peel
3	teaspoons basil	½	teaspoon dry mustard
1½	teaspoons pepper	6	oranges
2	cups honey	1½	teaspoons cornstarch
¾	cup butter	¼	cup cold water

Clean ducks; dry thoroughly inside and out. Combine 6 teaspoons salt with ginger, basil and pepper. Rub ½ seasoning mixture on inside of duck. Heat honey, butter, orange juice, lemon juice, orange peel, mustard and 1½ teaspoons salt together until butter melts. Rub 3 tablespoons of honey mixture inside each duck. Slice unpeeled oranges ½ inch thick. Stuff as many as possible in ducks' cavities. Pour 4 tablespoons of honey mixture into each duck. Truss ducks. Rub remaining seasoning mixture on outside of each duck. Individually wrap ducks in foil. Pour remaining honey mixture over ducks; wrap tightly and roast at 325° for 1¾ hours. Unwrap and baste ducks with drippings. Continue baking for 20-25 minutes. Remove ducks to platter and keep warm. Combine cornstarch with cold water; add to drippings. Stir and heat to boiling. Serve sauce with duck. Duck may be put on grill and basted instead of browning in oven. Serves 6.

Jean's Oyster Stew

2	tablespoons butter	2	tablespoons butter
1	pint oysters, undrained		Salt and pepper to taste
2	cups milk		Mace to taste
2	cups half-and-half	⅓	cup fine cracker crumbs

In top of double boiler, melt 2 tablespoons butter. Add oysters and juice. In saucepan, scald milk and half-and-half. Add 2 tablespoons butter, salt, pepper and mace. Slowly beat in crumbs. Pour into double boiler with oysters and let stand about 10 minutes. Warm before serving. Serves 6.

Wild Rice Casserole

8 ounces wild rice
6 cups water, divided
½ teaspoon salt
¼ cup onion, chopped
1 cup sliced fresh mushrooms

2 tablespoons butter
1 tablespoon plain flour
1 cup beef bouillon
⅛ teaspoon pepper
2¼ ounces sliced almonds

Wash rice under cold flowing water. Stir rice into 3 cups of water and parboil for 5 minutes. Remove from heat, cover and let rice soak for 1 hour. Drain and wash again with cold water. Cook parboiled wild rice in 3 cups salted, boiling water. Cover and cook 30 minutes or until nearly tender. Drain rice. Sauté onions and mushrooms in butter. Add flour and make a roux. Add beef bouillon and pepper; cook until smooth and thickened. Combine rice and vegetable mixture; pour into buttered 1½-quart casserole. Sprinkle with almonds. Cover and bake at 350° for 30 minutes. If too moist, remove cover and return to oven to let liquid absorb. Serves 6.

Tomatoes Stuffed with Spinach

6 medium tomatoes
10 ounces frozen chopped
  spinach
2 eggs, well beaten
½ cup cream of mushroom soup

1 cup grated sharp cheddar
  cheese
6 bacon slices, cooked and
  crumbled
Buttered cracker crumbs

Cut tops off tomatoes and scoop out pulp. Drain on paper towels. Cook spinach according to package directions; drain. Mix with eggs, mushroom soup, cheese and bacon. Stuff tomatoes with mixture and top with crumbs. Bake at 350° for 20-30 minutes. Chopped broccoli may be substituted for spinach. Serves 6.

Special Pecan Pie

½ cup sugar
2 tablespoons plain flour
  Pinch of salt
2 tablespoons butter
2 eggs, beaten
1 cup light corn syrup

1 cup pecan halves
3 ounces semi-sweet chocolate
  chips
1 9-inch deep dish pie crust
  Whipping cream, whipped

Mix sugar, flour, salt and butter. Add eggs and corn syrup. Stir in nuts and chocolate chips. Pour into unbaked pie crust. Bake at 350° for 45 minutes or until brown and set. Garnish each slice with whipped cream. Serves 6.

If only one oven is being used to prepare this menu be sure to complete cooking of the duck 30 minutes prior to dining. While keeping the duck covered and warm, use the oven to bake the tomatoes and rolls. Meanwhile serve the oyster stew as a first course to whet everyone's appetite for the feast to come.

Oktoberfest Feast

Serves 6

Herbettes
Hearty Reuben Pie
Haus Salad
Easy Butter Twist Rolls
Mountain Apple Torte

Herbettes

> 1 0.4-ounce package buttermilk
>   dressing mix
> ¾ cup oil

> 1 teaspoon dill weed
> 1 16-ounce box oyster crackers

Combine dry dressing mix with oil and dill weed. Put crackers into large plastic bag and pour dressing over them. Shake until crackers are well coated. Drain on paper towels. Yield: 6 cups.

Hearty Rueben Pie

> 1 9-inch deep dish pie shell
> 1 tablespoon caraway seeds
> ½ pound deli corned beef,
>   shredded
> 1 tablespoon Dijon-style
>   mustard
> ¼ cup Thousand Island dressing
> ¾ cup sauerkraut, drained

> 1½ cups grated Gruyere cheese
> 3 eggs, beaten
> 1 cup half-and-half
> 1 tablespoon grated onion
> ¼ teaspoon dry mustard
> ½ teaspoon salt
>   Kosher dill spears

Preheat oven to 425°. Sprinkle and press caraway seeds into pie crust. Prick crust and bake for 7 minutes. Remove crust and reduce oven temperature to 350°. Layer corned beef on top of crust. Mix mustard and dressing and spread over beef. Then layer sauerkraut and cheese. Mix eggs, half-and-half, onion, dry mustard and salt; pour evenly over pie. Bake at 350° for 40-45 minutes. Allow to set 5 minutes. Slice pie into 6 servings. Garnish each plate with a Kosher dill spear. Serves 6.

Haus Salad

Juice of 1 lemon
3 cloves garlic, crushed
1 teaspoon salt
½ teaspoon pepper
¾ cup oil
¼ pound bacon, diced

2 heads Romaine lettuce, torn
2 cups cherry tomatoes, halved
⅔ cup slivered almonds, toasted
⅓ cup grated Parmesan cheese
Salt and pepper to taste
1 cup croutons

To prepare dressing, mix lemon juice, garlic, salt and pepper. Beat continuously with fork while adding oil. Let dressing stand for 3 hours. Saute diced bacon until crisp; drain. In salad bowl, combine lettuce, tomatoes, almonds and bacon. Toss with dressing, Parmesan cheese, salt and pepper. Garnish with croutons. Serves 6.

Easy Butter Twist Rolls

6 tablespoons butter
1 10-count can buttermilk
biscuits

Sesame seeds

Place butter in 9x13x2-inch baking dish and melt in oven. Cut each biscuit in half. Twist each half several times, forming a corkscrew. Roll each twist in melted butter and arrange in baking dish. Sprinkle with sesame seeds. Bake at 425° for 8-10 minutes or until lightly browned. Yield: 20 rolls.

Mountain Apple Torte

⅔ cup plain flour
2¼ teaspoons baking powder
¼ teaspoon salt
2 eggs
1½ cups sugar
2 cups peeled and chopped
apples

1 cup chopped walnuts
1½ teaspoons vanilla extract
1 cup whipping cream
1 tablespoon rum

Preheat oven to 325°. Stir together flour, baking powder and salt; set aside. With whisk or fork, beat eggs and sugar until light. Add flour mixture and mix well. Stir in apples, walnuts and vanilla. Bake in greased 7½x11¾-inch baking dish for 40-45 minutes, or until top is crusty. Whip cream with rum. To serve, cut torte into 4x3-inch servings and garnish with whipped cream. Serves 6.

Oktoberfest has been celebrated in Greenville for more than ten years with Bavarian food, drink, music and dance. Sponsored by the Bavarian Festival Organization, the festival is held on two consecutive nights and attracts thousands of merrymakers. The tremendous success of the fall festival prompted the birth of a sister celebration, the Alpine Spring Festival, which is held in March and features different foods and music.

Christmas Goose Dinner

Serves 8

Canadian Goose
Butternut Squash Soufflé
Broccoli with Blender Hollandaise Sauce
Sherried Onions
Cheddar Biscuits
Trifle

Canadian Goose

1 8-pound goose	½ cup butter
1 quart buttermilk	¼ cup plain flour
1 8-ounce package prunes	Salt to taste
2 apples, sliced	1 cup goose broth
5 bacon slices	1 cup sour cream
Butter	4 tablespoons currant jelly

Soak goose in buttermilk overnight. Wash bird and drain. Preheat oven to 325°. Stuff cavity with prunes and apples; wrap goose with bacon. Wrap in heavy foil and bake for 3 hours. Baste every hour with butter. To prepare sauce, melt ½ cup butter in skillet. Stir in flour and salt; whisk until smooth. Add broth and heat, stirring constantly. Just before serving, add sour cream and jelly. Stir until smooth and serve with goose. Serves 8.

Butternut Squash Soufflé

2 cups cooked and mashed butternut squash	½ teaspoon salt
	1 teaspoon cinnamon
3 tablespoons butter, melted	½ teaspoon nutmeg
½ cup milk	3 eggs
1 cup sugar	1 teaspoon vanilla extract

Combine squash, butter, milk, sugar, salt, cinnamon and nutmeg; mix well. Add eggs, one at a time, beating after each addition. Stir in vanilla. Pour mixture into a greased 1½-quart casserole dish. Bake at 325° for 1 hour 15 minutes. Serves 8.

Broccoli with Blender Hollandaise Sauce

2 egg yolks	Cayenne pepper to taste
2 tablespoons lemon juice	½ cup butter, melted
½ teaspoon salt	1 large bunch fresh broccoli

Place egg yolks, lemon juice, salt and cayenne pepper in blender. Cover and mix well. Remove inner cap of cover and slowly pour in hot butter. Steam broccoli. To serve, pour warm sauce over broccoli. Serves 8.

Sherried Onions

6 medium onions
⅓ cup butter
½ teaspoon monosodium
  glutamate
½ teaspoon sugar
½ teaspoon salt
Pepper to taste
½ cup sherry
3 tablespoons grated Parmesan
  cheese

Slice onions into rings. Melt butter in large skillet; add onions, monosodium glutamate, sugar, salt and pepper. Sauté 5-8 minutes until rings are barely tender. Add sherry and cook 2-3 more minutes. Sprinkle with Parmesan cheese and serve. Serves 8.

Cheddar Biscuits

2 cups grated sharp cheddar
  cheese
¾ cup shortening
6 tablespoons cider vinegar
4 tablespoons ice water
2 cups self-rising flour
Dash of red pepper

Preheat oven to 425°. Cream cheese and shortening. Stir in vinegar and ice water. Stir in flour and mix with hands to form smooth dough. Roll out on floured surface to ½-inch thickness. Cut with 2-inch biscuit cutter. Bake for 10-12 minutes. Yield: 16 2-inch biscuits.

Trifle

4 cups milk
¾ cup sugar
4 eggs, beaten
Pinch of salt
1 commercial angel food cake
Sherry
1 cup whipping cream
2 tablespoons powdered sugar
1 pint fresh strawberries, sliced
½ cup chopped pecans

To prepare boiled custard, heat milk in top of double boiler. Add sugar to beaten eggs; add salt. Mix well. Add mixture slowly to warm milk. Stir constantly and cook until custard begins to thicken. When thickened, remove from heat and continue to stir for a few minutes. Chill custard. Break angel food cake into large pieces and sprinkle with sherry. Whip cream, adding sugar and sherry to taste. In large glass bowl, layer cake, custard, strawberries and cream until bowl is full. Top with pecans. Serves 12.

Break tradition from the expected turkey and dressing and serve this sumptuous Christmas buffet. Small wrapped gifts can double as place cards and will delight each diner.

Christmas Caroling Supper

Serves 12

Pizza Popcorn
Chicken Lasagna
Florentine Layered Salad
Italian Herb Bread
Cheddar Cheesecake

Pizza Popcorn

⅓ cup butter, melted
¼ cup grated Parmesan cheese
¾ teaspoon Italian seasoning
½ teaspoon salt
½ teaspoon garlic salt
10 cups freshly popped corn

Mix butter with cheese and seasonings. Pour over freshly popped corn in large shallow baking pan; mix well. Cook at 300° for 15 minutes.

Chicken Lasagna

12 ounces egg noodles
½ cup butter
½ cup plain flour
1 teaspoon salt
½ teaspoon pepper
½ teaspoon basil
4 cups chicken broth
5 cups cubed cooked chicken
3 cups cottage cheese
2 eggs, slightly beaten
8 ounces mozzarella cheese, grated
Parmesan cheese, grated

Cook egg noodles according to package directions; set aside. Melt butter over medium heat in sauce pan; blend in flour, salt, pepper and basil and cook until smooth. Slowly add broth and stir until sauce is thick and bubbly. Stir in chicken; set aside. In separate bowl, combine cottage cheese and egg; set aside. In 9x13x2-inch baking dish, layer as follows: ⅓ of chicken mixture, ½ of cooked egg noodles, ½ of cottage cheese mixture and ½ of mozzarella cheese. Repeat layers, ending with chicken mixture. Sprinkle heavily with Parmesan cheese. If ready to use, bake uncovered for 1 hour at 350°. May freeze. When ready to use, thaw casserole for 24 hours in refrigerator and bake uncovered at 350° for 1½ hours. Serves 12.

Florentine Layered Salad

3 cups torn raw spinach
Salt to taste
½ pound bacon, cooked and crumbled
Pepper to taste
1 tablespoon sugar
4 hard-cooked eggs, finely chopped
2 stalks celery, chopped
Salt and pepper to taste
3 cups torn lettuce
10 ounces frozen garden peas, thawed
3 tablespoons sugar
1 red onion, thinly sliced
2 cups mayonnaise
Paprika

Layer ingredients in large glass salad bowl in order listed above, except for mayonnaise and paprika. Ice salad with mayonnaise and sprinkle with paprika. Cover bowl tightly with plastic wrap; refrigerate all day or overnight allowing flavors to blend. Toss just before serving. Serves 12.

Italian Herb Bread

1 loaf unsliced Italian bread
⅓ cup butter, softened
1 teaspoon Worcestershire sauce
2 teaspoons dried parsley
½ teaspoon dried oregano
¼ teaspoon garlic powder

Slice Italian bread into 1-inch slices. Combine remaining ingredients, mixing well. Spread butter mixture between bread slices. Wrap loaf in foil. Bake at 350° for 20-25 minutes. Yield: 1 loaf.

Cheddar Cheesecake

6 ounces crushed Zweiback crackers
3 tablespoons sugar
6 tablespoons butter, melted
Grated rind of 1 lemon
32 ounces cream cheese, softened
8 ounces cheddar cheese, grated
1¾ cups sugar
3 tablespoons plain flour
5 eggs
3 egg yolks
¼ cup beer

Preheat oven to 475°. Prepare crust using crackers, 3 tablespoons sugar, butter and grated lemon rind. Press into bottom and 1 inch up sides of 9-inch springform pan. Chill. Beat softened cream cheese and grated cheddar cheese until smooth. Beat in sugar and flour; continue beating until light and fluffy. Add eggs and yolks one at a time, beating constantly. Fold in beer; pour into chilled crust. Bake at 475° for 12 minutes, then reduce heat to 250° and continue baking for 1½ hours. Turn oven off and let cake sit in oven for 1 hour. Do not open oven door until ready to remove. Take out of oven and cool to room temperature. Cover with plastic wrap and refrigerate. Serves 20-24.

Singing Christmas Tree Family Supper

Serves 8

Jenny Lou's Rump Roast
My Husband's Salad
Showhouse '84 Thousand Island Dressing
Squash Soufflé
Mushrooms and Rice
Drop Biscuits
Irish Apple Cake à la Mode

Jenny Lou's Rump Roast

2 tablespoons oil	3 medium onions, chopped
1 4-pound rump roast	Water
Salt and pepper to taste	¼ cup plain flour

Heat oil in 5-quart Dutch oven over medium heat. Liberally salt and pepper roast. Brown roast slowly for 20 minutes, turning occasionally to brown evenly. Add chopped onions and cook for 10 minutes. Add enough water to cover half the roast. Cover and continue to cook over medium heat for 2½-3 hours or until tender. Check roast occasionally to make sure it does not stick, adding enough water to keep meat half covered. When tender, remove roast to platter and let gravy cool slightly. Make a paste with flour and ½ cup water. Stir paste with fork until very smooth. Stir an additional 2 cups water into paste and blend well. Slowly add flour mixture to warm gravy and bring to a boil. Return roast to pan; cover and simmer for 30 minutes. Remove roast from pan; slice. To serve, arrange slices of roast on platter and top with gravy. Serves 8.

My Husband's Salad

3 bunches fresh spinach	½ cup croutons
1 head lettuce	6 bacon slices, cooked and
1 green pepper, chopped	crumbled
2 carrots, sliced	Parmesan cheese, grated
2 tomatoes, chopped	

Wash and tear lettuce and spinach. Toss together all ingredients except bacon and cheese. Just before serving, sprinkle bacon and cheese on top and serve with salad dressing. Serves 8.

Showhouse '84 Thousand Island Dressing

1 cup mayonnaise
¼ cup chili sauce
1 teaspoon paprika

2 hard-cooked eggs, grated
1½ tablespoons finely grated
onion

Mix well and refrigerate. Yield: 1½ cups.

Squash Soufflé

3 pounds yellow squash, sliced
4 tablespoons butter, melted
½ cup dried bread crumbs,
divided
½ cup chopped onion

2 eggs, beaten
1 teaspoon salt
1 teaspoon sugar
½ teaspoon pepper

Cook squash in water until tender; drain. Blend squash in a food processor
or blender. Melt butter and reserve for topping. Mix ¼ cup bread crumbs
with remaining ingredients and stir into processed squash. Pour into
greased 2-quart casserole. Top with remaining bread crumbs and drizzle
with melted butter. Bake at 350° for 1 hour or until bubbly. Serves 8.

Mushrooms and Rice

1¼ cups raw rice
2 10½-ounce cans beef
consomme
6 tablespoons oil

2 teaspoons instant onion flakes
2 tablespoons soy sauce
4 ounces sliced mushrooms,
drained

Mix all ingredients and pour into 1½-quart casserole. Cover dish and bake
at 350° for 30-45 minutes or until liquid is absorbed. To vary, omit onion
flakes, replace oil with 4 tablespoons butter and exchange 1 can of beef
consomme for 1 can of onion soup. Serves 6-8.

Drop Biscuits

1 cup commercial dry biscuit
mix

½ cup whipping cream
No-stick vegetable spray

Preheat oven to 375°. Stir biscuit mix and whipping cream to stiff
consistency. Drop by tablespoons onto baking sheet which has been coated
with no-stick vegetable spray. Bake for 12-15 minutes until browned. Yield:
1 dozen biscuits.

Irish Apple Cake à la Mode

1 cup oil
2 cups sugar
2 eggs
1 teaspoon vanilla extract
2½ cups plain flour
1 teaspoon salt

2 teaspoons baking powder
1 teaspoon cinnamon
4 cups diced apples
1 cup chopped pecans
12 ounces butterscotch morsels
Vanilla ice cream

Cream together first four ingredients. Add flour, salt, baking powder and cinnamon. Fold in diced apples and chopped nuts. Pour batter into greased and floured 9x13-inch baking pan. Sprinkle butterscotch morsels over mixture and bake at 350° for 50-60 minutes. Serve warm topped with scoop of vanilla ice cream. Serves 8-10.

The Singing Christmas Tree has been a showcase for talented youth in the Greenville community for more than 20 years. Annually more than 200 young people perform in this Christmas spectacular which traditionally opens Greenville's holiday season. The exceptional talent and unique performance format have resulted in national acclaim in recent years.

Elegant New Year's Eve Dinner

Serves 8

Tempting Tenderloin
Blender Bernaise
Tomatoes Stuffed with Mushrooms
French Onion Rice
Salade Carolina
Mimi's Rolls
Baked Alaska
Chocolate Sauce

Tempting Tenderloin

1 8-pound tenderloin
4 ounces Kitchen Bouquet
8 ounces commercial Italian
    dressing

2 cups herb seasoned stuffing

Trim tenderloin of all fat. Rub tenderloin liberally with Kitchen Bouquet and Italian dressing. Place meat in roasting pan lined with foil. Pour stuffing over loin. Place pan in cold oven. Bake for 30-35 minutes at 400°. Slice tenderloin to desired thickness and serve. Serves 8 .

Blender Bernaise

2 egg yolks
1 tablespoon lemon juice
1 teaspoon tarragon vinegar
1 teaspoon fresh tarragon leaves

1 tablespoon capers, drained
¾ cup hot melted butter
2 tablespoons fresh chopped
    parsley

Blend yolks, lemon juice, vinegar, tarragon leaves and capers in blender container. With blender running at low speed, gradually add ⅓ of butter in slow, steady stream. Turn blender to high speed; slowly add remaining butter. Fold in parsley. Serve immediately with meat, fish, or poultry. Yield: 1 cup.

Tomatoes Stuffed with Mushrooms

8 large tomatoes
1½ pounds fresh mushrooms,
    sliced
½ cup butter, melted
8 ounces sour cream
4 teaspoons plain flour

2 ounces Roquefort cheese
½ tablespoon dried oregano
1 teaspoon dried parsley
2 tablespoons dry sherry
Salt and pepper to taste

continued

Scoop out and drain tomatoes. Sauté mushrooms in butter until tender; drain and set aside. Combine sour cream, flour, cheese, oregano, parsley and sherry in saucepan and cook over low heat, stirring constantly until mixture is smooth and thickened. Add mushrooms, salt and pepper; stir well. Stuff tomatoes and bake in a shallow pan at 375° for 15 minutes. Serves 8.

French Onion Rice

1 8-ounce can sliced water chestnuts
8 ounces fresh mushrooms, sliced
1 cup butter, melted
2 10½-ounce cans French onion soup
2 cups raw rice
2 10½-ounce cans beef bouillon
¾ teaspoon salt
½ teaspoon pepper

Drain water chestnuts. Sauté water chestnuts and mushrooms in butter. Stir in remaining ingredients. Bake in covered 9-inch square baking pan at 300° for 1 hour. Serves 8.

Salade Carolina

2 teaspoons Dijon-style mustard
1 teaspoon English mustard
1½ teaspoons salt
½ teaspoon white pepper
2 teaspoons chopped chives
1 teaspoon Worcestershire sauce
½ cup fresh lemon juice
1 cup oil
¼ teaspoon dried basil
¼ teaspoon dried chervil
¼ teaspoon dried tarragon
1 14-ounce can hearts of palm
1 14-ounce can artichoke hearts
1 10½-ounce can asparagus spears
Mixed salad greens

Combine all ingredients except canned vegetables and salad greens. Mix thoroughly in blender. Refrigerate at least 3 hours before serving. Drain canned vegetables. On individual salad plates, arrange salad greens; top with hearts of palm, artichoke hearts and asparagus. Pour dressing over salad. Serves 8.

Mimi's Rolls

See Index

Baked Alaska

1 cup sifted cake flour	1 teaspoon vanilla extract
¾ cup sugar	¼ teaspoon cream of tartar
¼ cup cocoa	1 quart coffee ice cream
1½ teaspoons baking powder	2 egg whites
½ teaspoon salt	⅛ teaspoon cream of tartar
¼ cup corn oil	⅓ cup sugar
3 eggs, separated	⅛ teaspoon salt
⅓ cup milk	

Sift together flour, sugar, cocoa, baking powder and salt in large mixing bowl. Make well in center and add corn oil, egg yolks, milk and vanilla. Beat until smooth. In separate bowl, beat egg whites and ¼ teaspoon cream of tartar until mixture forms stiff peaks. Gently fold flour mixture into egg whites, blending well. Turn batter into 2 ungreased 8-inch cake pans. Bake at 325° for 20 minutes or until cake springs back when touched. Invert pans on rack; cool completely. Remove from pans by loosening sides with knife. Use one layer for Baked Alaska and freeze remaining layer for later use. Cover baking sheet with foil. Place cake layer on baking sheet. Mound softened ice cream evenly on top of cake, leaving ½-inch margin all around. Smooth surface with spatula. Place in freezer for 1 hour or until firm. Meanwhile, prepare meringue by beating egg whites and ⅛ teaspoon cream of tartar until soft peaks form. Gradually add sugar, 1 tablespoon at a time, and salt, beating until mixture forms soft peaks. Spread meringue over ice cream and cake, covering completely. Bake on lower shelf in 500° oven for 3-5 minutes or until lightly browned. Serve immediately with chocolate sauce. Serves 8.

Chocolate Sauce

4 ounces semi-sweet chocolate	¼ teaspoon salt
¾ cup water	1 tablespoon butter
¾ cup light corn syrup	1 teaspoon vanilla extract
½ cup sugar	

Heat chocolate and water in saucepan over low heat until chocolate is melted. Stir 10 minutes or until thickened. Gradually stir in corn syrup, sugar, salt and butter. Bring to a boil, stirring constantly. Remove from heat. Stir in vanilla; cool. Yield: 2 cups.

For a unique centerpiece saluting "Father Time," consider grouping a variety of tabletop clocks on a mirror or plateau. Festive curls of ribbon and lots of confetti complete the centerpiece. Incorporate your own touches of elegance to make the last night of the year an evening to remember.

Casseroles to Carry

Chicken Upside Down
Artichoke Chicken
Patio Beans
Strawberry Pretzel Salad
Autumn Cake

Chicken Upside Down

⅔ cup butter
⅔ cup plain flour
3 cups chicken broth
2 cups milk
1 teaspoon salt
½ teaspoon pepper
2 tablespoons lemon juice

2½ cups cooked cubed chicken
1 egg
⅔ cup milk
3 tablespoons oil
1 cup self-rising cornmeal
1 teaspoon sugar

Melt butter in pan over medium heat. Whisk in flour until well blended. Gradually add broth, then milk, seasonings and lemon juice. Cook sauce until thickened. Add chicken. Pour mixture into buttered 9x13x2-inch baking dish. The creamed chicken may be prepared ahead and frozen. When ready to serve, partially thaw and add cornbread topping. To prepare cornbread topping, mix together egg, ⅔ cup milk, oil, cornmeal and sugar. Pour over chicken and bake 40 minutes at 350° or until browned. Serves 8.

Artichoke Chicken

4 chicken breast halves, skinned
¼ cup oil
3 carrots, cut into 2-inch pieces
8 ounces fresh mushrooms, sliced
1 14-ounce can artichoke hearts, drained and halved
½ cup chopped green onion

½ cup sliced water chestnuts
¼ teaspoon dried whole thyme
½ teaspoon salt
⅛ teaspoon pepper
1½ cups chicken broth
½ cup sherry
2 tablespoons cornstarch

Brown chicken in hot oil in large skillet. Add carrots. Cover and simmer 5 minutes. Add mushrooms, artichokes, onion, water chestnuts, and seasonings. Cover and simmer 10 minutes. Preheat oven to 350°. Combine broth, sherry and cornstarch in a small saucepan; stir well. Cook over medium heat, stirring constantly until sauce is thickened. Place chicken and vegetables in greased 9x13x2-inch baking dish. Pour sauce over top. Bake covered for 20 minutes. Uncover and bake 40 more minutes, basting occasionally. Serves 4.

Patio Beans

4 bacon slices
3 medium onions, chopped
1 1-pound can pork and beans
1 1-pound can kidney beans
1 8.5-ounce can butter beans
½ teaspoon garlic powder
1 teaspoon dry mustard

½ teaspoon salt
¼ cup brown sugar, firmly packed
¼ cup vinegar
½ cup ketchup
½ teaspoon black pepper

Fry bacon until crisp; remove from pan. Sauté onions in bacon drippings. Combine all ingredients except bacon and place in 3-quart deep dish casserole. Cook uncovered at 350° for 45 minutes. Top with crumbled bacon and cook 15 minutes. Serves 8.

Strawberry Pretzel Salad

2⅔ cups broken pretzels
¾ cup butter, melted
1 cup sugar
8 ounces cream cheese, softened
1 2.8-ounce package whipped topping mix

2 3-ounce packages strawberry jello
2 cups boiling water
2 10-ounce packages frozen strawberries, thawed

Combine pretzels and melted butter. Spread in 9x13x2-inch baking dish. Bake at 350° for 10 minutes; cool. Cream sugar and cream cheese. Prepare whipped topping according to package directions. Mix topping with creamed mixture. Completely cover pretzel layer with mixture; refrigerate several hours. Dissolve jello in boiling water. Stir in strawberries and let cool. Pour over cheese layer and refrigerate. Cut into squares. Serves 12.

Autumn Cake

1 18-ounce can crushed pineapple
3 eggs
2⅔ cups sugar
1½ cups oil
3 cups plain flour
2 teaspoons cinnamon

1 teaspoon soda
1 teaspoon salt
1 teaspoon vanilla extract
1 cup shredded carrots
1 cup shredded coconut
1 cup chopped pecans

Drain pineapple and set aside. Combine eggs, sugar and oil in large mixing bowl. Sift flour, cinnamon, soda and salt together. Slowly add to egg mixture. Stir in vanilla. Add carrots, coconut, pecans and pineapple; mix well. Pour batter into greased and floured tube or Bundt pan. Bake at 325° for 1½ hours. Cool cake before removing from pan. Serves 20.

Super Bowl Cocktail Gathering

Serves 25

Glazed Beef Brisket
Missouri Mustard
Barbecued Turkey Breast
Easy Blender Mayonnaise
Pearl of the Sea Mousse
Layered Seafood Spread
Spinach Puffs
Vegetable Mélange
Chocolate Laced Fruit

Glazed Beef Brisket

1 8-pound beef brisket
2 lemons, sliced
4 oranges, sliced
4 onions, sliced

2 tablespoons pickling spices
⅔ cup brown sugar, firmly
packed
Assorted breads

Place brisket in Dutch oven; cover with cold water. Bring to boil and skim oil from water. Add fruit, onions and spices. Simmer 4 hours or until tender. Remove to roasting pan. Sprinkle with brown sugar and bake at 350° until sugar melts. Slice and serve with thin slices of assorted breads. Serves 25.

Missouri Mustard

3 ounces dry mustard
Apple cider vinegar

2 eggs, beaten
⅔ cup sugar

Put dry mustard in glass measuring cup. Add vinegar ¼ cup at a time, stirring continuously until mixture measures 1 cup. Cover cup and let stand overnight. Combine beaten eggs and sugar in top of double boiler. Add mustard mixture. Place over hot, not boiling, water and beat continually for 15-20 minutes or until thickened and smooth. Refrigerate in glass jar. Yield: 2 cups.

Barbecued Turkey Breast

See Index

Easy Blender Mayonnaise

1 whole egg
½ teaspoon dry mustard
½ teaspoon salt
2 tablespoons lemon juice

½ cup olive oil
½ cup corn oil
1 teaspoon water

Combine egg, mustard, salt, lemon juice, and ¼ cup olive oil in container of electric blender. Cover and blend at low speed. Uncover. With blender running, add remaining ¼ cup olive oil and corn oil in steady stream. Blend until thickened. Spoon into container. Add 1 teaspoon water to mayonnaise and mix well. The water serves to stabilize the mixture so that it will not separate. Yield: 1 cup.

Pearl of the Sea Mousse

6 hard-cooked eggs, chopped
1 cup mayonnaise
1 teaspoon salt
½ teaspoon pepper
1 envelope unflavored gelatin
2 tablespoons lemon juice
2 tablespoons water
1 teaspoon Worcestershire sauce

1 teaspoon anchovy paste
Dash of onion powder
1 4-ounce jar black lump fish caviar
Pimento strips
Black olives, sliced

Combine eggs, mayonnaise, salt and pepper in bowl; mix well. Combine gelatin, lemon juice, water, Worcestershire sauce, anchovy paste, and onion powder in saucepan. Cook at medium low, stirring until smooth and liquified. Combine gelatin mixture and egg mixture. Carefully fold in caviar. Decorate bottom of lightly greased 1½-quart ring mold with strips of pimento. Spoon mixture over pimento. Chill until firm. Unmold onto serving platter and garnish with black olives. Serve with unsalted round crackers. Yield: 1½-quart mold.

Layered Seafood Spread

8 ounces cream cheese, softened
1 tablespoon mayonnaise
¼ teaspoon Worcestershire sauce
Juice of 1 lemon
½ teaspoon seasoned salt
½ teaspoon lemon pepper
1 12-ounce jar cocktail sauce

¾ pound shrimp, boiled and peeled
½ pound Monterey Jack cheese, grated
3 green onions with tops, chopped
½ green pepper, chopped
½ cup sliced black olives
Salted crackers

continued

Mix cream cheese until smooth. Add mayonnaise, Worcestershire, lemon juice and seasonings. Spread evenly in a circle onto a round glass or silver serving platter. Refrigerate while preparing other toppings. Chop half the shrimp. Layer ingredients on top of cream cheese as follows: cocktail sauce, chopped shrimp, cheese, green onions, green pepper and olives. Arrange whole shrimp on top. This should resemble a pizza. Serve with salted crackers. Serves 25.

Spinach Puffs

2 10-ounce packages frozen chopped spinach
½ cup finely chopped onion
¼ cup butter
¼ cup plain flour
¾ cup milk

Nutmeg to taste
Salt and pepper to taste
½ pound cottage cheese
1 pound feta cheese
1 pound phyllo pastry
½ pound butter, melted

Thaw spinach; place on paper towels, and squeeze until barely moist. Sauté onion in butter until tender. Add spinach and cook over low heat, stirring constantly for 5 minutes. Add flour and milk; stir until blended. Season to taste with nutmeg, salt and pepper. Remove vegetables from skillet; cool. Add cheeses to spinach mixture; stir well. Cut sheets of phyllo lengthwise into 3½-inch strips. Working with one at a time, brush each phyllo strip with melted butter. Keep remaining strips covered, according to package directions. Place 2 teaspoons of filling at base of phyllo strip, folding the right bottom corner over it into a triangle. Continue folding back and forth into a triangle to end of strip. Place the triangles seam side down, on buttered baking sheet. Brush tops with melted butter. Bake at 350° for about 25 minutes or until triangles are well browned. Serve immediately. Yield: 60 triangles.

Vegetable Mélange

6 small zucchini
1 large head cauliflower
4 large carrots
25 small brussels sprouts
1 cup water
2 pounds fresh whole
green beans
1½ cups olive oil

¾ cup lemon juice
2 teaspoons salt
1½ teaspoons sugar
1½ teaspoons dried oregano
leaves
1 clove garlic, finely chopped
Leaf lettuce
8 ounces radishes

Cut zucchini in ½-inch slices. Cut cauliflower into bite-size florets. Cut carrots diagonally into ⅓-inch slices. In 3-quart saucepan bring 1 cup water to a boil. Add whole beans. Cover and simmer 10 minutes. Remove beans and drain. Cook remaining vegetables except radishes and lettuce, one variety at a time, until crisp tender. Drain each variety and place in plastic bag. Prepare marinade by mixing oil, lemon juice, salt, sugar, oregano and garlic. Divide marinade equally among vegetables in bags. Refrigerate vegetables, shaking bags occasionally. To serve, line serving tray with lettuce. Decoratively arrange each group of vegetables on lettuce. Garnish with radishes. Serves 25.

Chocolate Laced Fruit

2 cups mandarin orange
sections
2 cups pineapple chunks

2 pints large strawberries
16 ounces semi-sweet
chocolate

Drain canned fruit and pat dry on paper towels. Rinse strawberries, leaving stems intact. For best results, have fruit at room temperature for dipping. Melt chocolate over double boiler, stirring constantly until melted. Remove chocolate from heat and add ice cubes to water in double boiler to bring water temperature to warm. Dip each piece of fruit separately into chocolate, covering half of each fruit piece. Place on waxed paper. Let stand 10 minutes, until set. Prepare on day of party and refrigerate until ready to serve. To serve, arrange fruit decoratively on silver tray. Serves 25.

When decorating for your Super Bowl Cocktail Party, use the teams' colors in carrying out your theme and in your centerpiece. You might choose to decorate different rooms for each team's fans. For party favors, have a collection of visors, pompons, buttons or other football paraphernalia so guests can show their team loyalty!

Cocktail Bill of Fare
Serves 25

Tenderloin with Horseradish Spread
Chili Cheese Squares
Artichoke-Spinach Dip
Snow Peas Stuffed with Herb Cheese
Hickory Smoked Trout
Dill Sauce
Shrimp Piquante
Chocolate Glazed Toffee Bars

Tenderloin with Horseradish Spread

1 8-pound whole tenderloin	2 cups sour cream
1 15-ounce bottle	4 tablespoons prepared
Worcestershire sauce	horseradish
½ cup butter, softened	Salt and pepper to taste

Remove surplus fat and skin from tenderloin. Marinate in ½ bottle of Worcestershire sauce in the refrigerator for 5-7 hours. Coat sides of meat with softened butter. Place on broiling pan and broil on both sides, 6 inches from heating element, for 15 minutes per side. Remove from oven and leave at room temperature. Several hours before serving place seared meat in pan and pour remaining Worcestershire sauce over meat. Bake at 350° for 30 minutes. May leave at room temperature or refrigerate until serving. To prepare horseradish spread, mix sour cream, horseradish, salt and pepper. Refrigerate until ready to serve. To serve, slice meat thinly and serve with horseradish spread on small soft rolls. Serves 25.

Chili Cheese Squares

2 4-ounce cans green chilies	6 eggs
1½ pounds sharp cheese,	4 tablespoons sour cream
grated	Salt and pepper to taste

Halve green chilies and clean out seeds. Cut halves into strips and place them in bottom of 9x13x2-inch baking dish. Sprinkle grated cheese on top of chilies. Beat eggs; add sour cream, salt and pepper. Pour egg mixture over cheese and chilies. Bake at 325° for 35-40 minutes. Cool slightly and cut into squares to serve. Squares may be made ahead and frozen, then reheated in oven or microwave. Yield: 48 squares.

Artichoke-Spinach Dip

2 10-ounce packages frozen
  chopped spinach
1 small onion, chopped
1½ tablespoons butter
8 ounces cream cheese,
  softened
1 14-ounce can artichoke hearts,
  chopped

1 cup sour cream
1 cup mayonnaise
6 ounces mushrooms, chopped
Salt to taste
Red pepper to taste
Lemon juice to taste
Parmesan cheese, grated
Assorted crackers

Thaw and drain spinach thoroughly. Sauté onion lightly in butter. Mix all ingredients except Parmesan cheese and heat in double boiler. When ready to serve, sprinkle Parmesan cheese on top. Serve hot in chafing dish with assorted crackers. Serves 25.

Snow Peas Stuffed with Herb Cheese

50 snow peas
8 ounces cream cheese,
  softened
1 garlic clove, minced
2 teaspoons fresh chives,
  chopped

1 teaspoon dried basil,
  crumbled
½ teaspoon caraway seeds
½ teaspoon dried dill weed
½ teaspoon lemon pepper

Place snow peas in colander. Plunge basket into boiling water and remove immediately. Put snow peas in bowl of ice water. Split snow peas lengthwise. Blend remaining ingredients in food processor. Stuff small spoonful of mixture into each pea pod. Chill and serve. Yield: 50 pea pods.

Hickory Smoked Trout

4 whole rainbow trout,
  cleaned
Lemon pepper
1 cup lemon juice

1 cup soy sauce
Hickory chips
Fresh parsley
Lemon for garnish

Place cleaned trout in a dish. Leave heads, tails and fins on fish. Sprinkle generously with lemon pepper. Mix lemon juice and soy sauce; pour over fish. Cover and refrigerate overnight. Place trout on grill of a smoker. Follow directions for smoker and use hickory chips in the bottom. Smoke trout for 1½ hours or until fish flakes. Leave on smoker an additional hour after cooking so that fish will cool and come off grill easily. Chill thoroughly. Fish may be prepared up to 48 hours before serving and refrigerated. The trout can also be smoked, frozen and thawed. Before serving, cut skin carefully below gills and peel skin off both sides of each trout. Place whole skinned fish on serving tray and garnish with parsley and lemon twists. Use a small fork to flake the fish. Serve trout with a mild cracker and Dill Sauce. Serves 25.

Dill Sauce

1 cup sour cream
1 cup mayonnaise
2 tablespoons dill

$\frac{1}{8}$ teaspoon garlic salt
1 teaspoon lemon juice

Combine all ingredients and refrigerate. Serve as sauce with fish.
Yield: 2 cups.

Shrimp Piquante

5 pounds shrimp
  Crab Boil mix
1$\frac{1}{2}$ cups oil
$\frac{1}{2}$ cup ketchup
1 tablespoon Worcestershire
  sauce

7$\frac{1}{2}$ ounces prepared horseradish
1 8-ounce jar Dijon-style
  mustard
$\frac{1}{4}$ cup white wine vinegar
2 medium onions, thinly sliced
  Salt and pepper to taste

The day before serving, boil shrimp in crab boil for 5 minutes. Do not
overcook. Peel shrimp. Mix next 6 ingredients together for marinade. In a
covered bowl, layer shrimp with onions and sauce. Add salt and pepper.
Marinate shrimp in refrigerator, stirring every several hours. Remove shrimp
with slotted spoon and serve with toothpicks. Shrimp will keep several days
in the refrigerator. Serves 25.

Chocolate Glazed Toffee Bars

1 cup butter, softened
1 cup brown sugar, firmly
  packed
1 egg yolk
1 teaspoon vanilla extract

2 cups plain flour
$\frac{1}{4}$ teaspoon salt
6 ounces milk chocolate chips
$\frac{1}{2}$ cup chopped nuts

Combine butter, sugar, egg yolk and vanilla. Blend in flour and salt. Press
evenly in bottom of greased 9x13-inch baking pan. Bake at 350° for 25-30
minutes or until lightly browned. Crust will be soft. Remove from oven;
immediately top with chocolate chips. Cover with cookie sheet until
chocolate melts. As soon as chocolate is soft, spread evenly. Sprinkle
with nuts. While warm, cut into 2x1$\frac{1}{2}$-inch bars. Yield: 32 bars.

Poolside Cocktail Party

Serves 25

Saucy Appetizers
Hot Sour Cream-Pecan Spread
Southern Crab Dip
Asparagus Goodies
Mexican Hat Dance
Fruit-Cheese Tray
Chocolate Marbled Delights
Lemon Glazed Pecan Bars

Saucy Appetizers

2	pounds ground chuck	1	cup chopped onion
1	pound hot sausage	1	cup chopped green pepper
½	cup chopped onion	4	tablespoons butter
½	cup chopped green pepper	4½	cups ketchup
3	eggs	2	tablespoons mustard
1	package herb seasoned stuffing mix	4	tablespoons Worcestershire sauce
2	teaspoons salt		Garlic salt to taste
½	teaspoon pepper	1	cup brown sugar, firmly packed
1	tablespoon soy sauce	2	tablespoons white vinegar
2	tablespoons Worcestershire sauce		

Prepare meatballs by mixing the first 10 ingredients together in a large bowl. Make into balls and brown in skillet. Drain. To prepare sauce, sauté onion and green pepper in butter until tender. Add remaining ingredients; simmer for 20-25 minutes. Add meatballs to sauce; simmer an additional 20 minutes. Can freeze meatballs in sauce. Serves 25.

Hot Sour Cream-Pecan Spread

24	ounces cream cheese	¾	teaspoon pepper
6	tablespoons milk	1½	cups sour cream
3	2½-ounce jars dried beef	1½	cups chopped pecans
¾	cup chopped green pepper	6	tablespoons butter
6	tablespoons onion flakes	1½	teaspoons salt
1½	teaspoons garlic salt		Triscuits

Combine cream cheese and milk. Tear beef into small pieces and combine with pepper, onion flakes and seasonings. Add to cream cheese mixture; mix well. Fold in sour cream. Spoon into 9x13x2-inch baking dish. Brown pecans in butter and salt; sprinkle over sour cream mixture. Bake at 350° for 30 minutes. Serve hot with Triscuits. Serves 25.

Southern Crab Dip

1¼ cups mayonnaise
⅔ cup sour cream
2¼ tablespoons French dressing
1¼ teaspoons horseradish
2½ teaspoons Worcestershire
   sauce

¼ teaspoon salt
⅛ teaspoon pepper
1 pound sharp cheddar cheese,
   grated
2½ pounds crab meat
   Butter-flavored crackers

Blend together mayonnaise and sour cream. Add French dressing, horse-radish, Worcestershire sauce, salt and pepper. Mix in cheese and crab meat. Stir lightly and refrigerate. This should be made one day in advance. Serve with butter-flavored crackers. Serves 25.

Asparagus Goodies

½ cup butter
3 ounces blue cheese
1 ounce cream cheese
2 tablespoons sour cream

20 slices white bread
1 19-ounce can asparagus spears
3 tablespoons melted butter
   Parmesan cheese, grated

Cream butter with blue cheese, cream cheese, and sour cream. Remove crust from bread slices. Roll each slice of bread with rolling pin until flat. Spread cheese mixture lightly over each slice of bread. Drain asparagus and place on paper towel until dry. Place one asparagus spear on each bread slice. If asparagus is too long, cut off large end. Roll bread around asparagus spear. Place on cookie sheet, seam side down. Cut each in half. Drizzle melted butter over top of rolls. Sprinkle Parmesan cheese over each roll. Bake at 350° for 15-20 minutes or until browned. Yield: 40 goodies.

Mexican Hat Dance

4 ripe avocados
   Juice of 1 large lemon
½ teaspoon salt
¼ teaspoon pepper
2 1.25-ounce packages taco
   seasoning mix
2 cups sour cream

4 16-ounce cans refried beans
4 tomatoes, chopped
8 green onions, chopped
3 cups shredded lettuce
1 4½-ounce can ripe olives,
   chopped
1 pound cheddar cheese, grated

Peel, pit and mash avocados with lemon juice, salt and pepper. Combine sour cream and taco seasoning mix. To assemble, spread beans on 2 large shallow serving platters; spread seasoned avocado mixture over beans; spread sour cream mixture over avocado mixture. Sprinkle tomatoes, onions, lettuce and olives over all. Cover with grated cheese. Serve chilled or at room temperature with tortilla chips. Serves 25.

Fruit-Cheese Tray

1 half-pound wedge Jarlsberg
  cheese
1 half-pound wedge Gouda
1 half-pound wedge Brie

1½ pounds seedless green grapes
1 pound red grapes
3 kiwi, peeled and sliced
12 thin breadsticks

Arrange the fruit, cheeses and breadsticks attractively on a round tray. Serves 25.

Chocolate Marbled Delights

16 ounces semi-sweet chocolate
¾ cup butter
8 eggs
3 cups sugar
1 tablespoon vanilla extract
½ teaspoon almond extract
2 cups plain flour
2 teaspoons baking powder
2 teaspoons salt

2 cups chopped pecans
12 ounces cream cheese,
  softened
½ cup butter, softened
1 cup sugar
4 eggs
2 teaspoons vanilla extract
¼ cup plain flour

Melt chocolate and butter in double boiler. In large bowl beat eggs. Gradually add sugar until mixture is thick and light in color. Blend in chocolate mixture. Add vanilla and almond. Combine flour, baking powder and salt and stir into chocolate mixture. Stir in nuts. To prepare cream cheese filling, blend cream cheese and butter; add sugar and mix well. Add eggs one at a time, beating well after each addition. Add vanilla and stir in flour. Grease two 9x13-inch baking pans. Divide chocolate mixture between pans, reserving 4 cups for top layer. Spread cream cheese mixture evenly in pans. Top each with 2 cups of chocolate mixture and marble. Bake at 350° for 30 minutes or until tester comes out clean. Yield: 8 dozen.

Lemon Glazed Pecan Bars

1½ cups plain flour
½ cup butter
½ cup brown sugar
2 eggs, beaten
1 cup brown sugar
2 tablespoons flour
1½ cups flaked coconut

1½ cups chopped pecans
½ teaspoon baking powder
¼ teaspoon salt
½ teaspoon vanilla
1 cup powdered sugar
  Juice of 1 large lemon

Combine first 3 ingredients and put into 9x13x2-inch glass baking dish. Bake at 275° for 8-10 minutes. Cool. Combine eggs and brown sugar; mix well. Set aside. Combine flour, coconut, nuts, baking powder and salt. Mix well with egg and brown sugar mixture, then stir in vanilla. Spread over cooled crust Bake at 350° for 18-20 minutes. Combine remaining ingredients and drizzle over top while hot. Cut into bars when cool. Yield: 54 1x2-inch bars.

NOTES

Recipe Index

Almonds

Amaretto

Appetizers and Hors d'Oeuvres

Apples

Apricots

Artichokes

183

184

185

189

Recipe Contributors

Greenville Junior League Publications would like to thank the members of the Junior League of Greenville, Inc. and other friends whose contributions of recipes created this book and its standard of excellence.

Johanna Corbin Aiken
Jeanie Reuell Alexander
Mary Ann Harper Allen
June Barton Anderson
Mary O'Dell Ashmore
Lila Doody Barr
Salley Langley Batson
Eydie Bohler Baucom
Elizabeth Wertz Beacham
Penny Prout Beacham
Jean Leatherwood Beech
Martha McAngus Belcher
Patricia Hutchison Bethea
Susan Nicholson Blythe
Ellen Rushing Boan
Mary Price Bolt
Myra Huffstetler Bonner
Chan London Boyd
Scottie Lu Parker Brandt
Sarah Wightman Brice
Elizabeth McLeod Britton
Margaret Mardre Brockman
Lynn Pruitt Brown
Jarrell LaGrone Bruner
Jean Leatherwood Buck
Lane Weaver Byrd
Jennie Gaines Caldwell
Cathryn Holman Callahan
Lynn Edmonds Campbell
Mary Schuyler Campbell
Jenny Gordy Cannon
Virginia Livie Cansler
Jo Catherine Carpenter
Carolyn Harris Carroll
Lisa Brennan Cash
Nancy Pierce Cashwell
Donna Bartholomew Cheves
Kay Wyatt Cheves
Sue Woods Chittenden
Fran Coker Clark
Jill Rushforth Coker
Claudia Barton Coleman
Malinda Moore Coleman
Judith Cope Colovin
Cokey Still Cory
Libby Farnham Crabtree
Carrell McCaskill Cranswick
Beth Watson Croft
Cheryl Benson deHoll

Mary Gillespie Dellinger
Effie Beattie Dickey
Karen Coogler Dobson
Jean McSween Donkle
Christy Holliday Douglas
Patricia Robinson Dowling
Burnley Kinney Dunlap
Elizabeth Leman Dunson
Merle Engel Dunson
Casey Case Durham
Becky Cowell Edmonds
Anne Southerland Ellefson
Lacy Casteel Ellis
Laura Ann Forrester Ellison
Myra Wofford Elmus
Carol Inglett Evans
Claudia Houser Fant
Lee Jones Farrar
Happy Claiborne Faust
Ann Richert Ferrell
Maribeth Gardner Finley
Wendy Geanne Frantz
Leslie Shirley Fricke
Ranette Miller Gaffney
Betty Cook Garrison
Barbara Emmel Geiger
Robin Brownlee Giddings
Jane Williams Glenn
Joy Davis Glenn
Susan Scales Glenn
Sandy Scott Goodwin
Ellen Jennings Gower
David Benjamin Gray
Elizabeth Cann Gray
Joyce Gaston Gray
Nell Johnston Gray
Georgea McKinley Greaves
Jo Anne Moseley Hammond
Tracy Timmons Hardaway
Karen Herring Harmon
Joey Cotten Harris
Henry Long Harrison
Pat Manly Harrison
Dorothy Merry Haynsworth
Mary Ann Hernak
Diane Wynsen Hickey
Alice Ann Domingos Holman
Sherry Blatt Hooper
Marianne Hyland Hornak

Eunice Rice Horton
Diddy Forrester Hughes
Mary Cary Hughes
Velda Carter Hughes
Stella Martin Hungerford
Helen Horton Hunt
Mary Jane Gilbert Jacques
Betty Webb Jelks
Ann Martin Jennings
Nancy Thayer Jennings
Elise Wall Johnson
Catherine Spence Jones
Ann Farrish Justice
Joan Dew Kellett
Lydia Willard Kellett
Karen Spencer Kelsey
Day Newton King
Pam Reeves Knight
Katherine Richards Knox
Lisa Gooch Koehler
Lucy Simpson Kuhne
Martha Dunson LaGrone
Carol Wienges Laffitte
Sarah Prude Leinweber
Harriet Leister Ligon
Lucinda Ann Lion
Berkeley Haynsworth Little
Betsy Bomar Littlejohn
Alice Casteel Lonnecker
Elizabeth Snow Mann
Barbara Watson Maroney
Gladys Grier Marshburn
Ann Beacham Martin
Deborah Webster Martin
Dewanda Flora Martin
Susan Jones Martin
Cathy Stall McCall
Deborah Gibson McCauley
Esta Bradley McCrary
Eleanor Thomas McCullough
Ruth Alford McDonald
Vicky Guess McDonald
Susan Brigham McKibbon
Emma Cothran McMahan
Cathy McGee Mebane
Paula Starr Melehes
Joyce Mellman
Cathy Cleveland Melnyk
Crickett Robbins Merritt

Bonnie Pietsch Mitchell
Margaret Ann Jones Moon
Carol Brandenburg Morgan
Grier Gower Mullens
Fitzie Carroll Mumford
Haley Pyle Nations
Leonette Dedmond Neal
Barbara Marshburn Nickles
John Keneth Nickles
Mary Ann Mellen Noot
Ann Lowe Nuckolls
Lei Williams Offerle
Carolyn Lee Orders
Diana Schmitt Orders
Nora Carruthers Outten
Elaine Brooks Paine
Margaret Kinley Parham
Betty McClenaghan Pearce
Susan Gray Pinson
Ginny Lou Piper
Heather Hylton Poe
Ames Longstreet Post
Val Jackson Post
Margaret Aiken Praytor
Florence Gillem Pressly
Evelyn Woodford Prince
Anseleene McLendon Prout
Ann Foster Provence
Leslie Scoles Provence
Louise Albright Quinn
Raymond Crawford Ramage, Jr.
Dorothy Peace Ramsaur
Pamela Hodge Ramseur
Marguerite Manning Rasor
Martha Hudgens Reed
Jackie Graham Reynolds
Claire Fontaine Rice
Elizabeth McDonald Richardson
Catherine Robbins
Frances Hill Roe
Page Lonnecker Rogers
Peggy Pinson Rogers
Mary Ann Mellen Root
Antoinette Carson Rothfus
Marti Doyevarr Rounsville
Lynn Foushee Rowell
Becky Stowe Ruff
Caroline Albright Ryan
Sharon Preston Schlosser
Minor Mickel Shaw

Ann Cheves Sherard
Carol Sharpe Short
Betsy Clary Smith
Nancy Orders Smith
Sara Stephens Smith
Carolyn Schoepf Spigner
Betty Peace Stall
Louise Williams Stanford
Sharon Schoenwalder Steinmann
Dianne Asbill Stephenson
Mary Peace Sterling
Caroline Batson Stewart
Carolyn Godwin Stirm
Elizabeth Jervey Stone
Furman Ivey Stone
Vee Reinhardt Stone
Ginger Menges Stuart
Gladys Gray Sullivan
Kay Williamson Sullivan
Jane Brewer Sykes
Maye Webb Foster Tatum
Martha Laurens Taylor
Betty Heath Teague
Iris Tewksbury
Kay Trowbridge Thomas
Ruth McKeithan Thomason
Sidney Rutledge Thompson
Sherri Ratley Timmons
Julie Woodfin Toledano
Nancy Masker Toole
Elizabeth Gaines Van Doren
Maggie Echols Wade
Pamela Rushmore Wagner
Harriet Riley Watkins
Harriett Stuckey Watson
Margaret Saye Watson
Sherrill Altman Whetsell
Sallie Peterson White
Jenny Fallis Widmer
Patty Patterson Willett
Anne Aichele Williams
Lucille Giles Williams
Sydney Timmons Williams
Cathy Suddeth Wilson
Caro Wyche Wofford
Marcia Moorehead Workman
Harriet Smith Wyche
Cindy Higgins Young
Jane Sperling Young

Testing Committee

Greenville Junior League Publications would like to thank our Testing Committee for its dedication and contributions of time, talent and money in the creation of these quality menus.

Johanna Corbin Aiken
Eydie Bohler Baucom
Penny Prout Beacham
Elizabeth McLeod Britton
Lynn Pruitt Brown
Rosemary McKinney Brunson
Lynn Edmonds Campbell
Mary Lee Bettis Cantey
Cynthia Leigh Carson
Frances Coker Clark
Jill Rushford Coker
Stephanie Lewis Cornwell
Kristina Davis
Christy Holliday Douglas
Merle Engel Dunson
Gaye Farr Dupree
Helen Case Durham
Joan Johnstone Edwards
Anne Southerland Ellefson
Carol Inglett Evans
Lee Jones Farrar
Karen Cothran France
Harriett Boyd Funk
Robin Brownlee Giddings
Susan Scales Glenn
Ellen Jennings Gower
Liz Cann Gray
Tracy Timmons Hardaway
Karen Herring Harmon
Patricia Manley Harrison
Anna Striplin Hill
Linda Ericson Hill
Catherine Spence Jones
Karen Spencer Kelsey
Pam Reeves Knight
Leslie Helen Lehr
Sara Prude Leineweber
Nell Conger Lucius
Susan Jones Martin

Cathy Stall McCall
Deborah Gibson McCauley
Cricket Robbins Merritt
Barbara Marshburn Nickles
Alice Barron Pearce
Jane Eatman Piper
Heather Hylton Poe
Margaret Aiken Praytor
Jane Sullivan Price
Pamela Pace Pritchett
Leslie Scoles Provence
Natalie Townsend Putman
Gladys Ruth Rice
Candy Sommer Richardson
Elizabeth McDonald Richardson
Sharon Preston Schlosser
Greg Schneider
Minor Mickel Shaw
Carol Sharpe Short
Nancy Orders Smith
Sandy Ray Spann
Carolyn Schoepf Spigner
Dianne Asbill Stephenson
Martha Laurens Taylor
Kay Trowbridge Thomas
Sherri Ratley Timmons
Jane Brenegar Trexler
Pam Rushmore Wagner
Margaret Saye Watson
Sherill Altman Whetsell
Debbie Nye Whittle
Jenny Fallis Widmer
Harriet Arnold Wilburn
Patty Patterson Willett
Sydney Timmons Williams
Cathy Suddeth Wilson
Caro Wyche Wofford
Martha Farrell Wrenn
Cindy Higgins Young

Greenville Junior League Publications Steering Committee

Anne Southerland Ellefson
Tracy Timmons Hardaway
Sally Jameson Henley
Diddy Forrester Hughes
Beth McDonald Richardson

Martha Laurens Taylor
Margaret Saye Watson
Sallie Peterson White
Leigh Glenn Zimmerman

Uptown Down South Creative Staff

Edie Bohler Baucom
Ellen Jennings Gower
Tracy Timmons Hardaway
Susan Jones Martin
Barbara Marshburn Nickles

Beth McDonald Richardson
Martha Laurens Taylor
Sherri Ratley Timmons
Margaret Saye Watson
Jenny Fallis Widmer

Greenville Junior League Publications gratefully acknowledges the following individuals:

Harvey C. Dellinger — Creative Director
Wes Walker — Photographer
Jim Banks — Stylist
Kathey Hartman Livengood — Word Processor
Carol Seigler Hastings — Word Processor

Greenville Junior League Publications expresses special thanks to friends who assisted the *Uptown Down South* Staff in proofing this publication.

Penny Prout Beacham
Emmy Aichel Dawson
Anne Southerland Ellefson

Lisa Gooch Koehler
Ann Beacham Martin
Patty Patterson Willett

Greenville Junior League Publications gratefully acknowledges the following businesses:

Leatherwood, Walker, Todd & Mann
Hale's Jewelers

Rich's
The English Way

GREENVILLE JUNIOR LEAGUE PUBLICATIONS